Pigeon Showing

Douglas McClary

Pigeon Showing

BLANDFORD PRESS
POOLE · DORSET

First published in the U.K. 1984 by
Blandford Press, Link House, West Street,
Poole, Dorset BH15 1LL.

Copyright © 1984 Blandford Press Ltd

Distributed in the United States by Sterling
Publishing Co., Inc., 2 Park Avenue,
New York, N.Y. 10016.

British Library Cataloguing in Publication Data

McClary, Douglas
  Pigeon showing
   1. Homing pigeons—Showing
  I. Title
  636.5'96   SF469

ISBN 0 7137 1372 0

Typeset in 10/12 Plantin by
Megaron Typesetting, Bournemouth

Reproduced, printed and bound in Great Britain by
Hazell Watson & Viney Limited,
Member of the BPCC Group,
Aylesbury, Bucks

Contents

Preface

The showing of pigeons is a hobby which continues to increase in popularity throughout the world. Competition is international for racing pigeons, with Olympiads being staged in different countries and teams competing from many parts of the world, the language barrier seeming to hold few problems for the fanciers attending.

Pigeons are kept just about everywhere and, wherever they are kept, there will be pigeon shows. Having travelled in several countries and attended countless pigeon shows, I have been aware for some time of the dearth of written material on the showing of pigeons. Novices can have a difficult time gaining knowledge and expertise, and it is with this in mind that I decided to write this book to explain some of the aspects of the sport.

Bearing in mind the countless and varied breeds of pigeons which are shown, the task was a daunting one, owing to the necessity of avoiding catering for some instead of the vast majority. Most of my involvement with pigeons has been with the showing and racing of pigeons, although I have shown breeds and been involved in general pigeon showing for many years. I have therefore tried to avoid talking about the need of the show racers and the racers and to generalise in such a way that any fancier wishing to compete at pigeon shows will have a form of reference. I have aimed at the middle of the road, although I suspect that it will be the novice fancier who will find the contents most useful.

I am also conscious that I am writing primarily for British and North American readers, and therefore fanciers from other parts of the world will have to bear this in mind, especially in chapters where the times of the year are mentioned. It would be impossible to cover the subjects without some reference to climatic and other conditions.

The writing of this book has been a pleasure and I hope that it will supply enjoyment to pigeon fanciers for some time to come. I am grateful to my wife Ann, for her tolerance and assistance, to Ruth Turl who has also worked at the typing aspect, and to the staff of the *Racing Pigeon*, London for their guidance.

Pigeons are kept for pleasure by people all over the world but so much more enjoyment can be gained by showing them. Pigeon showing is a wonderful hobby and will continue to grow just as the leisure time available to us all also continues to expand and I hope this book will fill a gap in the written word on the subject and encourage even more people to enjoy their pigeons.

Douglas McClary
Exeter, 1984

Chapter 1

Making a Start

The acquisition of the skills required to show pigeons successfully demands an untiring amount of energy, patience and perseverance. In a book such as this, it is not an easy task to offer advice on the best way to make a start, bearing in mind that there are hundreds of different breeds of pigeons which can successfully be shown. However, I will deal with the subject in as general a manner as possible, and hopefully by so doing the information will pertain equally to the show racer, the pigmy pouter, the nun, the jacobin, or almost any breed of show pigeon. A great deal will depend upon how the fancier's introduction to the sport has been made. However, I feel that I must confine myself to two main avenues: (a) the complete novice and (b) the more experienced fancier who is either returning to the sport after an absence or who is changing his breed.

In most cases, people thinking about showing pigeons have made up their minds as to the breed or breeds they wish to keep. This probably applies even to the novice, whose introduction will either be through attendance at a show, where admiration has been extended to some of the birds there, or through a friend who happens to be a fancier. If the breed has been chosen, then the general advice which follows will apply but the problem of the person who is looking for a suitable breed to keep, enjoy and ultimately show is quite different.

This would-be fancier will have to apply his mind to exactly what he wants out of his pigeons. If he wants them for flying ability then he will doubtless have to think towards racing pigeons, show racers, flying tipplers, Birmingham rollers, West of England flying tumblers or one of the breeds mainly designed for fast, high or performing ability. This presents a fairly simple choice and generally these breeds are very hardy and easy to keep and rear.

If, however, thoughts are towards breeds for decorative purposes, then the possibilities are numerous and it would be far beyond me to offer advice in any particular direction. Of course, some of the purely fancy breeds are capable of flying out and the pigmy pouters and larger croppers which I have seen on the wing present a particularly fine spectacle, as well as having a great deal of character in and about the loft. There are, however, so many breeds to choose from and almost each and every group of pigeon has its own attractions, as well as pitfalls and difficulties in breeding, and advice on such matters can only be gained from those with the most experience in the breeds.

The advice, therefore, for someone who is still looking for a suitable breed is to attend as many shows and to visit as many fanciers as possible in order to gain as wide a cross-section of knowledge, information and advice as is available. There is no substitute for attendance at the large classic-type shows for here most of the breeds are exhibited at their best and there is also a good guide as to the competition available within those breeds. There are, however, a number of specialist books on the market, some dealing with particular breeds but others of the encyclopaedia type, giving details of each of the breeds in turn with a pen picture of each. Weekly and monthly magazines are also available and likewise give good information to the would-be buyer, as well as offering birds for sale from time to time.

The most experienced fancier will most certainly have chosen the breed on which he wishes to concentrate and will therefore be in a more fortunate position, not only having a better understanding and knowledge of his desires within that breed but also a better idea of where to go to acquire his stock. He will also know the difficulties which can be experienced and, hopefully, will be in a better position to plan against them. However, from this point onwards, let us assume that the fancier has decided upon his breed. Generally birds will be purchased in one of the forms described below.

(a) *Stock or Breeding Birds* It is certainly most useful to be able to buy stock birds or stock pairs from any experienced fancier. In so doing, one is not only buying birds capable of breeding good youngsters for future shows but in some way buying the experience of the fancier concerned because if they, with that experience, have seen fit to keep birds for their stock value, then undoubtedly there has been good reason. Indeed, it may be possible to buy pairs or single birds from successful fanciers within the breed and thus quickly have a good breeding stud. Providing that the birds are not too old for breeding purposes and one can anticipate a year or two of successful breeding from them, these will always give good value for money. There is also the breeder's pride of producing one's own team from such purchases.

Stock birds obtained from clearance sales following deaths or complete disposal will most certainly give very good value because generally the older stock pigeons can be purchased at considerably less cost than those fit for immediate show.

(b) Show Pigeons It is always most tempting for the newcomer to a breed to purchase winning show pigeons from a successful exhibitor. Whilst this has considerable advantages in allowing the fancier to be able to show right away, it must be remembered that the successful pigeons are not necessarily the best for breeding purposes and they will most certainly cost a great deal more than stock birds. Many fanciers are unwilling to part with their winning stock, unless paid considerable sums, as they fear that they will be beaten by their own pigeons at future shows. A lot, however, depends on the cash available and someone with this as a minor consideration might well be able to spend money and produce an instant show and probably breeding team at the same time.

(c) Young Birds, Late-breds or Eggs Most experienced fanciers will help newcomers by giving them a start within the sport. After all, the future of the sport depends on the availability of new fanciers coming into it and the manner in which most will be persuaded to help out is either by the supply and sale of young birds throughout the breeding season or by extending their breeding season slightly to rear up a round of late-bred pigeons. Some even prefer to give or sell a few eggs but this system is rather fraught with difficulty and chance and, of course, depends on the availability of birds able to sit the eggs in question.

Young pigeons throughout the season, of course, are a good bet because the purchaser is not only purchasing a ready-made young show team but also availing himself of the experience of the fancier concerned because his experience has gone into the production of the young birds in question. Late-breds also present an attraction in that they are generally cheaper and, given time, will develop just as well as any other pigeon. A lot depends on just how late in the season they are bred but, if they are bred in sufficient time, they will have a complete and full moult and thus be available for show towards the end of the first season and then for the following full season.

(d) Complete or Part Team From time to time, there will become available full or part teams owing either to the death of fanciers or their desire to dispose completely of their pigeons or of a particular breed. This is the ideal way for any fancier, whether novice or experienced, to gain an immediate foothold in any breed. Such opportunities should be taken, even if the outlay at the beginning is considerable, because once again experience and knowledge has been bought at the same time as the pigeons. Such sales are often also accompanied with other advantages, for example, the sale of

appliances such as baskets or other show containers, drinkers and other pigeon equipment. In some cases, the fancier's breeding and show record of a long standing may also be available.

As stated, this is the most advantageous way of getting into a breed but it must be realised that such opportunities are few and far between.

One consideration which should always be applied when contemplating showing a particular breed is the competition which is available. It is, for instance, pointless to pick a breed which is extremely rare and has very limited showing opportunities. It is appreciated that such pigeons can always be entered in 'any other variety classes' but this is not a very satisfactory way of showing as breed competition is at its best when against other representatives of the breed and not totally unrelated types of bird. Such rare breeds may be useful as second or third breeds but if one is serious about showing then consideration should be given to the purchase of a breed where there is ample availability, competition and numbers of shows to be entered. It is most certainly worth applying a great deal of thought to this particular point.

Another matter to be considered in the early stages, especially where it is difficult to acquire more than a small number of the breed concerned, is to have a number of pairs of feeders available, such as racing pigeons. Feeders can mainly be purchased quite cheaply, or even acquired from the fanciers wishing to dispose of surplus stock, and, in the early stages of the production of the family, their services can be invaluable. I can best conclude by giving some very general advice which will apply in most cases:

(a) Attend as many shows as possible, especially the larger ones, to study, question, query and gain advice.

(b) Get to know as many successful fanciers as possible.

(c) Purchase from as few sources as possible. It is always a mistake to buy here, there and everywhere for the chances of blending the purchases together into a compact family unit are more remote. Far better to buy from one, two or three sources only.

(d) Do not go in for too many breeds. The ideal is to concentrate on one only, although in the fancy breeds and where varieties are concerned, there is always a temptation to diversify; most certainly for the novice there should be an aim to keep to one or two breeds only.

(e) Purchase pigeons from fanciers who have a distinct and close-knit family of pigeons if at all possible. Good and successful families will have been bought only after a great deal of work and study and one is more likely to be able to breed birds of quality from such purchases than from fanciers who give little time or consideration to the production of their own strain or family.

(f) The most expensive is not necessarily the best. Be prepared to back one's own judgement in appreciating the value of stock acquired from genuine and dedicated fanciers.

Chapter 2

Housing of Show Pigeons

A great deal has been written on housing for pigeons, but the vast majority of this applies to lofts for racing pigeons, with much of the emphasis being placed upon trapping arrangements. Indeed, modern thought has concentrated to a large extent on how to get the racers into the loft in the quickest possible time, so as to save valuable seconds at the conclusion of a race. Open-door trapping (Figure 1) is now very much favoured, especially by those who use the widowhood system of racing.

It follows, therefore, that most of the proprietary lofts advertised throughout the world are aimed at racing enthusiasts, for obviously these are most numerous and where the best market is to be found. However, much can be gained by making a study of racing lofts for they have much to offer by way of imagination, style and practicability.

When we talk about housing for show pigeons, however, we are into a different set of needs, with good, secure and settled housing being the main consideration and less emphasis being required on thoughts of trapping. Many breeds of pigeon other than the racers, however, have need to be liberated, either for free-flying or into a flight or aviary, and this particularly applies to show racers and the fancy flying breeds.

I have always found the subject extremely interesting for there are very few lofts which are similar to any other and each and every fancier has set ideas on the ideal sort of housing for his breed of pigeon. I suspect also that I am not alone in being constantly on the watch for better ideas than my own, and in constantly changing the design or fittings in and around my lofts.

Over the years, I have owned several lofts in various shapes and sizes and perhaps in this way I have reasonable experience of some of the problems to be found. All my working life I have been subject to moving about and this has resulted in problems which do not often face the average fancier. Perhaps, therefore, before I mention specific aspects, I can recount some of my trials and tribulations in pigeon-housing and these might then relate better to some of the observations I will be making later.

My main interest has always been in showing and, with my nomadic style of life, perhaps it is just as well because problems with racing

Figure 1. A typical garden loft. Note the low-level ventilation louvres, the use of adjustable glass louvres and the orderly 'V'-perches. Birds enter through the open door. There is no landing board because the birds go straight to their perches.

pigeons would have been much greater. I first kept pigeons when a young schoolboy in Cornwall and it was a once-and-for-all fascination. My first pigeons were housed in a converted rabbit hutch and here I enjoyed my first pleasure in keeping and caring for pigeons.

I soon realised that my pleasure could be heightened considerably by being able to get in with the pigeons and very soon I talked my father into relinquishing half of the chicken house, giving me considerable room and the ability to multiply numbers kept. The birds were soon flying out, giving great pleasure. Soon the chickens were further relegated and my pigeons reigned supreme!

My early showing was conducted from that structure, for the mere desire to keep pigeons soon deepened into one to keep beautiful ones. Despite the severe limitations of the building, I seem to recall rearing good youngsters and turning out some good show prospects. However, schooldays came to an end and work away from home forced the disposal of the birds.

For a number of years, I was out of pigeons and it was not until my marriage that the opportunity arose for me to keep pigeons again. My great fear in those days was the prospect of having to move house so consequently my thoughts were to have a very small loft, very portable

15

and convenient. I, therefore, commenced with a shed 7×5 feet (2.1×1.5 metres) in area, divided into two, and this served me for a couple of seasons before necessity proved it to be too small for one with serious showing in mind. Various methods of increasing its size were used, such as adding bays, then an aviary, but I soon realised that a larger loft would be the only answer.

My next choice was a purpose-built loft, size 10×6 feet (3×1.8 metres), divided into two sections and with a bay running almost the full length along the front. Apart from problems of keeping the driving rain out, this proved to be an excellent loft and it served me well for a number of years.

My moves were becoming a little less frequent and my enthusiasm for showing became an obsession, so much so that I commenced looking towards a third compartment. I therefore purchased a large garden shed capable of division into three compartments, each with a bay to the front. Again, it gave me considerably more flexibility and I enjoyed my pigeon fancying greatly from it. However, an inevitable move showed me the inadvisability of such a structure, for all the conversion work had considerably reduced the portability aspect and its dismantlement and re-erection was a nightmare.

Plans were immediately made for the purchase of my present loft, a purpose-built 18×6 feet (5.5×1.8 metres) wooden loft. The end of the story? Not quite, for although it has withstood well two removals to its present location, I have made several alterations to it over the years, changing the plain front to one with bays and glass louvres, and also made other minor adjustments, such as to the end housing the doorway.

I am now left with a loft of that size, neatly and conveniently divided into three equal 6×6 feet (1.8×1.8 metres) compartments. The internal partitions are solid boarded, except for the sliding doors which are half dowelled and, being the exact size, are bolted to both the front and rear walls of the loft, adding greatly to the strength of the structure overall. It has proved to be a very good and convenient show loft. I still think of improvements I could or would like to make and am now planning a new loft of three compartments but with a service corridor running along the entire front, providing access to each of the compartments.

What therefore are the main considerations for a suitable loft for show pigeons? In the knowledge that trapping arrangements can play a less important role, I consider that the following will form the main aspects for decision.

(a) The size of loft required and the space available for it.

(b) Its functional value in line with the type of bird to be kept.

(c) Its appearance – to be as pleasing as possible.

In his book *The Pigeon,* the late Wendell M. Levi stated that he considered the main considerations to be the comfort of the pigeons, the convenience of the fancier and the cost. I would not disagree with these sentiments, for all manner of considerations have to apply.

Certainly the aim must be to provide a home for the pigeons which will allow them to settle into a happy and contented environment and so be able to produce excellent condition for shows. This is most certainly the important aspect as far as the showing of birds is concerned and most fanciers, I think, will agree that fancier comforts will take second place to such an important matter.

For instance, there are many examples of fanciers who have started out with unambitious and ordinary buildings, but have been able to produce superb and successful teams of pigeons. They have then decided to invest in a more pretentious structure and found that success has dwindled, owing to the birds enjoying their new abode less. The wise fancier is the one who appreciates the reasons for his success and plans in and around his existing arrangements.

Considerations for show pigeons will therefore depend on the type of breed to be kept. Large birds will require more space than the miniature varieties. Fanciers entering a particular breed will of course have taken note of the normal type of housing employed by the successful fanciers within the breed and will probably cater accordingly. What is required for genuine homers, jacobins, runts or other large varieties, may well be most unsuitable for Chinese owls and the like.

With size in mind, thought will be given to the number of compartments requirement for management. I believe that, wherever possible, at least three should be sought. This provides for considerable flexibility to plan for a show team throughout the twelve months, allowing separate compartments for cocks and hens and one for young birds; the breeding compartment should be in either of those set aside for the cocks or hens. If a small team only is kept, it may well be that, during the show season when the sexes are separated, the third compartment can be left spare for the erection of show pens, thus allowing a penning room.

A word of warning at this point, however, about size and the number of compartments. There is no substitute for time spent by the fancier in the loft, so that any division of that total may be reflected in the overall management. For instance, one compartment means that the fancier's

Figure 2. View of corridor loft showing adjustable glass louvres to regulate the air flow.

entire time in the loft is spent with all the birds; two compartments result in a halving of the time with the birds, and three or more compartments result in further divisions of the time available to the birds. It follows that fanciers with more than one team or loft lose out in the overall time with each bird. It is worth thinking about when forming the initial plans.

Let me return to the size of the compartments, especially the width from back to front. For small breeds, 5 feet (1.5 metres) may be adequate but for show racers or anything larger, I would always recommend at least 6 feet (1.8 metres). The width from side to side depends again not only on the size of the bird but on the numbers wanted to be kept. Perch sizes and spacing will depend upon the size of the bird and a 4 feet (1.2 metres) wide partition may be far too narrow for the majority of breeds.

To return to my own loft, with the 6-feet (1.8 metres) square compartments depending on the size of the birds, I can have banks of box-perches either six or seven wide, and four deep, allowing for either twenty-four or twenty-eight birds in each compartment, as an absolute maximum. With a very small breed, I might be able to extend the perching to eight or even nine wide.

I have always admired those with lofts which are large enough to allow for a corridor running the length, outside of the various

Figure 3. Inside a corridor loft. Note the facility to service the drinkers and food trays from the corridor.

compartments (Figure 2). These allow the fancier access to be able to study the birds in their various divisions, and yet not cause them to be unsettled by actually entering with them. Indeed, many extend this facility so that the feeding and watering can be done from the corridor area. Bathing can also be done in this area, thus ensuring that the floor of the compartment area is kept dry.

In my planned loft, I am considering a structure 8 feet 6 inches (2.6 metres) in width, with 2 feet 6 inches of that being used as a service corridor along the front. This system has much to commend it and I have included a photograph (Figure 3) to show a typical example. The corridor acts as 'fancier space', allowing movement without inconvenience to the birds. In lofts such as mine for instance, to get to the end compartment, access is only through the other two areas.

I would now like to expand a little on what Levi saw as one of the main considerations – the convenience of the fancier, when one determines the position of a loft. This does require a great deal of thought regarding its location near to existing services, footpaths and clear areas. This will apply to fanciers with lofts in their own gardens (Figure 4), and cannot do so to all those countless fanciers who are forced to keep their birds in groups of lofts on allotments of ground, well away from their own houses.

In my early days, I bought sheds with ridge-type roofs, which allowed me to place the door on either end, depending on any new house and garden I lived in, so that it could be placed to face the

Figure 4. An elaborate American loft, the property of Mr. E. L. Robbins of Kentucky.

Figure 5. Loft bay with bath underneath.

nearest pathway, etc. An available supply of clean water is a
consideration, as is the nearness of the electricity supply. A quick trip
to the loft is made a chore if the loft is sited well away from the house
and possibly at the top or bottom of a steep slope.

The aim should be to make the relationship between fancier and
pigeon a happy and relaxed one. A little thought at the planning stage
will do much to bring this about.

If a corridor is not possible, it might be worthwhile thinking about
adding bays to the front of the loft. I currently have one fitted for each
of the three compartments (Figure 5). These have aided management
considerably, giving the birds more access to direct sunlight and by
allowing the drinking vessels to be located there. In my own cases, and
I have seen them used in the same manner elsewhere, I have the baths
placed under the floor of each bay.

Providing baths, therefore, becomes less of a chore, being simply a
case of lifting the removable floor, pouring in the water and allowing
the water to drain afterwards.

The bays also add space to a loft, giving extra space and another area
in which to fly and alight. They really do aid management and can be
recommended.

So far I have said little about ventilation, yet I regard it as being one
of the most important factors in getting the environment right within
the loft. It is most important to have adequate ventilation so that the air
is clean at all times. It is important also, however, to ensure that
draughts are avoided, especially the direct ones bearing the cold winds
– mainly the Easterlies.

I have seen racing lofts where there is so much wire on all sides that the wind is allowed to blow directly through. I cannot imagine that this is conducive to good condition or happiness on the part of fancier or birds. For show pigeons, however, the need is for dry, clean, well-ventilated and regulated air space.

Ventilation generally means allowing a space for air to enter at low level and be able to leave the loft at a higher level – usually at roof height. It is very important that this air escape should allow the escape of foul air, but not allow direct draughts in. The object is to be able to regulate the air stream to allow for and compensate for the vast differences in temperature throughout the year.

This can be achieved by the use of opening windows, either hinged or completely removable, or as in my case with the use of adjustable glass louvres. These have proved to be a great asset in allowing natural sunlight in, keeping out cold winds, but opening in hot conditions to allow in the maximum amount of air.

At one time, the manufacturers of pigeon lofts seemed to pay scant regard to the provision of ventilation, but are now alive to the need and provide low-level intakes – generally by louvres – and foul air escapes. I can now relate back to my first ever loft – the chicken house – which served me so well. In those days, I did not think a great deal about ventilation, but now, on reflection, realise that it was provided through the spaces left because of the use of a corrugated roof covering.

All talk of ventilation brings me most conveniently to the position of the loft and the direction of the compass it should face. I can say without doubt, that a great deal depends on getting this right. I always advise that lofts should face the South to attract the sunshine for the majority of the day. Sunshine rays are beneficial to most forms of life, killing germs and reducing the chances of disease.

The main disadvantage is that much of the rain comes from the South and as a result thought will have to be given to making waterproof the fronts of lofts so facing. The direction is right not only for attracting the maximum amount of sunlight, but also in countering the cold winds. My present loft faces East and is in its third location. The two previous ones were South-facing and I now know that the birds were better in that loft in those locations. Even when writing this chapter, I am contemplating re-locating the loft to a Southerly aspect. It is in its present position owing to it being the most convenient for appearance, the presence of paths and its position being clear of shrubs and trees.

I realise that it has been a hard way to learn a lesson but I feel that I have proved that ventilation suiting a loft in one position will be no earthly good if the loft is placed to face in another direction. A South-facing loft will hardly be affected by Easterlies, but my loft catches them full in the face, and also fails against the Northerlies.

A settled environment is absolutely essential to be able to produce birds in show condition. It is of course a much easier matter to assert than to produce. The fancier, by his very demeanour, will do much to allow or prevent birds settling, but the very nature of the building will have a considerable effect.

The bird must have a love of its home, a psychological attitude which is almost impossible to define in such a way as to be able to bring it about with any certainty. The fancier may well have to experiment with the structure available to him – to add to or reduce the light, improve or reduce the ventilation, perhaps enlarge the compartment or perch sizing or spacing. These are the variables which go to make up the whole.

Birds which fly out are better for it. I can say that in the sure and certain knowledge that it is true, having seen racers given 'open loft' and by witnessing the improvements to health and vigour as a result. Therefore, I would always advise fanciers to allow their birds their liberty wherever possible, not only for the acknowledged flying breeds, bur for others not so noted for their flying ability. I have a view that too many fancy breeds are treated as cage birds as opposed to pigeons.

Where free-flying is not possible, then there should be an aim to build a flight or aviary large enough for the birds to have a reasonable fly, but whatever, to be able to get out into and to enjoy the sunshine. Baths can be administered in the flight area, resulting in happy, fit pigeons, and this will be shown in fitness and the realisation of show condition.

If neither course is available, then it should be possible in some way to allow birds access to the light and sunshine by constructing bays or at the least by arranging perches allowing access.

So far, of course, I have confined my remarks almost entirely to portable buildings. Perhaps this is due largely to my own experience and needs over the years. Before turning my thoughts to alternatives, I will try to illustrate my problems by relating a particularly difficult removal over a distance of nearly a hundred miles.

The move had to take place in April, right in the middle of the breeding season. All my breeding was being done in portable and self-contained nest boxes in pairs. When the time came, the breeding pairs were shut into their respective boxes, together with their eggs or youngsters. The boxes were then stored in the garage overnight. The loft was then dismantled and loaded on to a van. When everything else was loaded the following day, the nest boxes and occupants were also loaded, and the lot taken to the new address.

Figure 6. Exterior view of a typical European roof-top loft. In the roof can be seen two look-outs and four trap-openings – one for each racing section in the loft.

The boxes were the first off the van and placed on a lawn in the sunshine while the loft was erected on its new site. This done, the birds in their boxes were placed back in the loft and the sole damage consisted of one broken egg, all other eggs and youngsters surviving the experience.

At one of my addresses, I had access to a brick-built summer-house which I converted to house my pigeons – or some of them. I constructed a wooden floor about 12 inches (30 cm) off the concrete floor and produced a loft which proved to be an excellent one. The brick walls did much to maintain a mean temperature over most of the year, giving little change to the conditions being experienced by the birds. It was a successful venture and I was sorry when I had to move.

The majority of pigeon lofts must be of a portable nature, but as always there are some wonderful exceptions where considerable sums of money have been spent in the production of 'pigeon palaces'. The European countries, and Belgium and Holland in particular, have many such wonderful lofts, often to be found in the roof area of the main residence (Figure 6).

Such structures are ideal for both pigeons and fanciers. I would love to experience such conditions but feel that this is a state which will always be beyond me. Brick or block-built lofts must be ideal for maintaining a good average temperature for the birds, a state which can be maintained by artificial means if necessary.

Much innovation has been applied to some of the modern lofts, especially those which are commercial in nature. Mesh floors, steam cleaning, constant running water, heat in winter, forced air in hot conditions, are but a few of those being applied to further the sport. From these ventures, of course, will come modifications which will suit the average fancier, and by so doing benefit the sport as a whole, so anything to enhance the sport should always be encouraged and not decried.

However, to return to the portable lofts. Wood is by far the most common material used and I have seen metal and aluminium sheds used to good effect and also concrete section. The latter is heavy and subject to condensation. This brings me on to the subject of suitable roofing material.

Most of my portable lofts were roofed with wood covered in the rubberised felt material which grew brittle with time and then needed replacement. I now keep my wooden roof but cover it with either a corrugated asbestos or metal material and this has proved to be very successful. However, such materials, used without the wood cover or some other form of 'skin', result in condensation during damp climatic conditions and will do harm to the show candidate inmates.

I would now like to mention the appearance of our pigeon lofts. In the past, the pigeon fanciers of the world have been given a 'working man and cloth cap' image and to some extent this has been injurious to the pigeon in society. Demeanour of fanciers has had much to do with this, but also the state of pigeon housing, which has often been dilapidated and hardly pleasing to the eye.

I think that it is in the best interest of all to try to present our pigeon houses in as good an eye-pleasing way as possible. A cleanly painted or well-finished loft, kept clean and pleasant, is good for the sport and this should be the aim of pigeon fanciers everywhere.

Personally, I would never paint the outside of another loft. It is time-consuming and an ongoing chore. It looks good when first done, but when in need of repainting, can look terrible. I would always advise that a newly constructed wooden loft should be treated with a suitable wood preservative, allowing the natural grain of the wood to remain and to allow it to blend in with the surrounding environment. Even a large loft such as mine can be treated in a matter of an hour or so, and relatively cheaply. Painting the same loft would take days.

Likewise, I do not paint the inside of my lofts, preferring the natural wood, which can be quickly and easily scrubbed periodically to maintain its good appearance. Painting inside is even more laborious and can take days to do, and days to dry safely for the birds to be able to return. None of that problem in my lofts with natural wood.

In conclusion, I would like to offer this as advice to any fancier contemplating the purchase or construction of a new loft. It is to visit as many fanciers as possible in order to glean ideas and ideals. From them, learn the ideal, then temper it to fit the cash available. This sounds a simple matter, but I would go further, by advising that one should afford more than what seems affordable! The best is always the cheapest in the long run, so aim high!

The plan should include the observations of other fanciers, coupled with the need felt by the fancier as to how he intends keeping the breed in the future – not in one year, but in five years when more fully established. The better and closer to the ideal in loft construction, the easier it will be to achieve success with the birds in the loft.

If the loft allows the fancier, by its suitability and practicability to produce, develop and maintain a set pattern of management, then it is doing its job in providing the pigeons a good residence with settled conditions and, by so doing, provides the fancier with a foundation for successful showing.

Chapter 3

Accessories for the Show Loft

Just as a great deal of thought is necessary to produce the ideal type of loft, it is also necessary to consider at length the internal design and fittings, as well as the accessories to be used therein.

Most of the items mentioned are necessary as a means of applying day-to-day maintenance but the majority will also aid the management of the pigeons. The requirements for the show pigeon are little removed from those of the racing pigeon, so that most accessories and fittings can be purchased from normal suppliers. The differences in design will have to be tailored to meet the particular needs of the breed to be kept in the loft, with size being the guide.

However, the internal design of any loft reflects the fancier and his management and one can tell a great deal by a study of lofts and inmates. I am bound to admit, however, that the fancier and his methods are most important in any loft, for the expert will control his pigeons whatever the fittings inside.

Perches

We all have our own ideas on the ideal type of perch and here, right away, it is possible to see wide differences. Over the years I have tried all sorts but have always returned to the straightforward box perch. I believe these to be suitable for most breeds of pigeons, having used them for all the birds I have ever kept, and as we are primarily talking about show pigeons, I feel sure that they are best suited for showing purposes.

There are variations on box perches, i.e. those with sloping bases on blocks for the birds (Figure 7) but overall, the rows of box perches are neat, presentable and extremely practical. Their size can be tailored to suit the breed to be kept, with allowances for the large and well-feathered varieties and small boxes for the small breeds. Size will be suited to the breed, for management success depends much on the control given by optimum size. The show racer is the breed I am most connected with and here I believe that 10 inches (25 cm) is an ideal width, with about the same in height. I have used larger ones but have found that control tends to suffer as a result of the boxes being too large.

I also favour perches on only one wall of each compartment as a

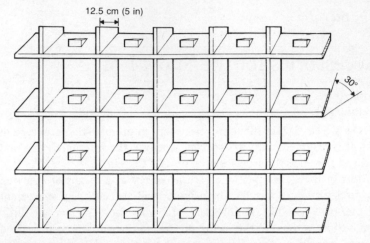

Figure 7. *Box perches with sloping face and block.*

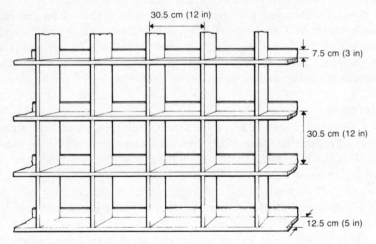

Figure 8. *Box perches showing backing battens.*

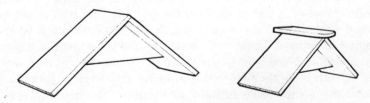

Figure 9. *'Saddle' or V-shaped perches.*

28

means of making cleaning easier. I dislike birds perching all over walls, above doors and so on.

My own box perches are all backed by a strip of wood approximately 3 inches (7.5 centimetres) in height (Figure 8), again to assist in cleaning and also to keep the walls of the loft cleaner. My perches are normally 2 to 3 inches (5 to 7.5 centimetres) off the wall, leaving additional space for the tail and feathers to spread and for the bird to turn but many fanciers board the rear of the perches. This has some points to commend it, in giving additional privacy to the inmate, and in keeping out draughts which may come in from behind, e.g. through the foul air escape.

The other form of perch most favoured seems to be the 'V'-type (Figure 9), in vertical rows. The shape provides some protection to the birds in the lower perches and again provides a neatness which appeals to me. However, I can find little else to commend 'V'-perches except that they can be made by even the most amateur of carpenters. They do not provide sufficient protection to the birds using them and, as a result, marauding pigeons can have a field day, fighting for perches and thus leading to a falling-off in condition and the possibility of broken flights or other feathers – not to mention the soiling of feathers.

Nest Boxes

Boxes which are permanently fitted within pigeon lofts can aid management considerably and most racing lofts favour this arrangement (Figure 10). Birds tend to retain their own boxes throughout the year and the breeding season is therefore considerably aided by this. Usually the boxes are in the cocks' section and, in many cases, the only perches are those provided by the boxes or the flaps on the nest fronts.

The main advice regarding nest boxes is to have them as large as possible. Breeding can be made so simple if the boxes are large enough for the birds to be able to remain in their boxes if necessary. Work is involved in the feeding and watering but the main advantage is in the certainty of parentage. I, therefore, feel that anyone planning the construction of nest boxes should have them just as large as space allows.

Certainly in racing pigeon circles, the provision of nest boxes has received great prominence, owing to the growing use of widowhood systems of racing. However, the type of box used, capable of division into two, has a lot to commend in show pigeons, allowing two rounds to merge well. It is another example of where the ideas of one section of the sport can aid others.

Owing to my nomadic style of life, I have always been forced to use

Figure 10. A well-ordered loft interior with widowhood nest boxes. Note the raised drinking vessel and the sliding roof for ventilation.

Figure 11. Bank of three nest boxes with recessed fronts. The recess provides a shelf on which food and water pots can be placed and the low-level entrance allows the young birds to leave the nest and observe the outside world.

31

portable boxes (Figure 11) and these have served me well. In fact, in the previous chapter, the advantages during one removal operation are described. However, they are convenient to use and after use can be scrubbed, allowed to dry in the sunshine and then are easily stored until required the following season.

One of the main advantages in using portable boxes is that they can be placed in varying places in the loft, reducing the chances of birds entering boxes by mistake. I tend to place the boxes on different walls, and even at varying angles to give relief to the surroundings. The birds seem to like this especially the boxes which tend to provide privacy. Privacy can be aided also by screening the nesting area within the nest box with hardboard, or by putting smaller cardboard boxes in the nest boxes. I appreciate that the placing of the nest boxes goes against my usual desire for uniformity in appearance but I feel that it is worthwhile for the relatively short period of the breeding season when contentment is all important for good strong youngsters to be produced.

If portable boxes are to be considered, then why not disposable ones, made out of either cardboard or hardboard. These could be either purpose-made, or use could be made of existing boxes – tea-chests and the like. The big advantage here is that they can all be burned at the conclusion of the season, meaning less work and less chance of disease.

Partitions

These are the main part of the permanent internal fittings to a loft. In the past, many lofts were divided using dowelled or lathed partitions, with the result that the birds could see each other, including cocks and hens. I cannot believe that this is a good thing, especially for the show candidates. I therefore favour the use of close-boarded partitions and mine are so constructed. They are boarded except for the sliding doors in each, which are half-dowelled to aid the free flow of air. As already stated, the partitions are strongly built to the exact size of the loft interior, adding strength to the whole building.

Fanciers may well require that their partitions be made removable so that small compartments can be joined for the breeding season. This idea has a lot to commend it and is seen as a means of using the partitions to assist in the general management.

Doors

All my internal doors are sliding ones and I like them very much. Until a year or so ago, my exterior door was also of a sliding variety but I dispensed with it when I discovered that field mice were able to gain access to the loft by squeezing through the gap between door and loft.

Sliding doors have a lot of advantages in that they take up less room and are not liable to blow open, as is the conventional hinged door. Security is the only problem in that it is far more difficult to find locks for sliding doors. Security is after all a most important consideration in loft design and management.

Nest Bowls

Over the years, the earthenware types have been most popular, being easy to clean and store, and they are economical owing to their long life (Figure 12). Nowadays, however, the compressed paper disposable ones are gaining in popularity and have much to commend them, including ease of disposal after use. They are reasonably priced and provide warmth through insulation. Even better insulation is provided by polystyrene bowls, which are slightly more expensive but quite popular.

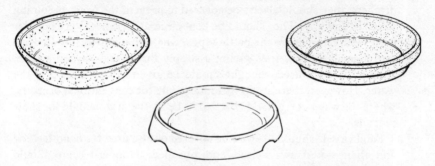

Figure 12. A selection of nest bowls. These may be manufactured in earthenware, papier-mâché or plastic.

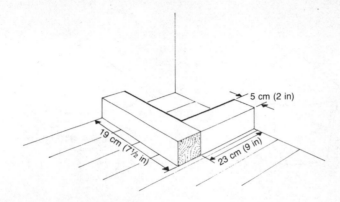

Figure 13. A simple makeshift nest base.

Fanciers who are able to allow their birds open loft will tell you that no nest bowl is required because their birds will find enough material to build large nests which provide safety for the eggs and youngsters. My team of racers will work all day carrying sticks and twigs into the loft and this also has the advantage of giving them exercise and happiness.

I often supply a make-shift appliance which can act as a nesting base consisting of two pieces of timber joined (Figure 13) and the birds are very happy with these. The timber should be heavy enough so that there is no fear of tipping, but most birds will quite happily build a nest within the confines of the frame. The half-squares will last for years, can be creosoted after cleaning and are easily stored.

Drinking Vessels and Food Appliances

These take numerous forms (Figures 14 & 15) and can be purchased at any supplier of pigeon products or even pet stores. With regard to drinkers, they should always be covered to prevent the water becoming soiled in any way. They should be kept clean at all times. Very popular with some fanciers are the bottle types, where the bottled supply drips into a small shallow tray, giving a supply for several days at a time. Where these are used, thought should be given to sterilisation of the water. However, there seems little substitute for conventional drinkers, where the water is regularly changed as being the best method for show pigeons.

Food vessels should likewise be covered or else used for hand-feeding and then stored away clean and unsoiled. Hopper-feeders should always be covered and, where this method is used, extra care should be taken to keep vermin out of the loft. Grit also should be placed in dry, clean containers (Figure 16) which should be covered wherever possible.

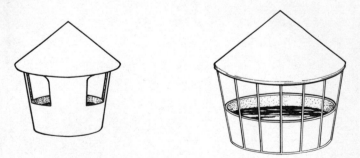

Figure 14. Drinking vessels. The lids protect the contents from droppings.

34

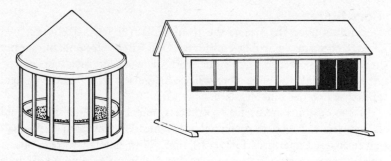

Figure 15. Feeding vessels.

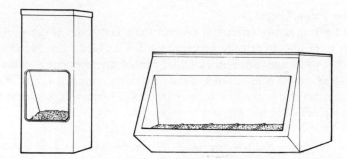

Figure 16. Grit containers.

Baths

In the previous chapter, I mentioned the provision of baths under bays of the loft as being a method advised. However, baths for pigeons come in all shapes and sizes and much will depend upon the size of the breed kept. Galvanised metal baths (Figure 17) have been favoured for many years and can be purchased at pigeon sundry suppliers, as can the more modern plastic varieties, some with drain plugs.

There are many useful receptacles about nowadays, including the polythene or heavy plastic butcher's or fish merchant's trays. These make ideal baths for pigeons.

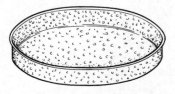

Figure 17. Galvanised metal bath.

Corn Storage

Depending upon the size of the team kept, it is most likely that two sizes of corn storage will be employed. One will be a reasonable supply held in the loft itself, in some sort of wooden, metal or plastic container, while the main store will be held elsewhere – in the garage, outhouse or other suitable place.

Plastic dustbins are useful receptacles, metal coal bunkers also hold fair amounts. I tend to prefer wooden chests for my corn with small gauze-covered apertures for ventilation. With enough storage space, the main reserves can be so held and turned into the required mixture for transfer to the loft store for convenience as and when required.

Show Pens/Cages

Any aspiring showman should possess show pens/cages (Figure 18) in order to be able to provide pen training for his birds. I would almost say that pens/cages form an essential part of management in order to train birds to the pen well before their first ever outing to a show. Pens or cages can also be used for other purposes of loftmanship, such as the isolation of new or sick pigeons.

Figure 18. A show bird being trained to the pen. Few showmen have a separate penning room but all must be able to get the young birds used to the show pen.

The real luxury is in having a penning room, properly fitted out. It is then possible for one's birds to be penned on the occasion of visits from other fanciers, as a means of training and also for an independent judgement of their potential as future show specimens. This will particularly apply to the training and selection of young birds.

Baskets and Crates

Any showman must possess proper containers for the conveyance of birds to and from shows. They should be divided into compartments, one for each pigeon, giving it sufficient space to be comfortable and to have plenty of air, but not so large as to make its journeys tiring through being thrown about.

Sizes are fairly well prescribed and the crates and baskets supplied (Figures 19, 20 & 21) will suit most of the varieties of pigeons shown. I have always favoured the use of wicker baskets (Figure 19), having found them reasonably priced, long-lasting, good-looking and comfortable for the birds. They are slightly larger than the aluminium or plastic crates (Figure 20) on the market today and therefore less easy to pack into cars or other confined spaces, but their advantages are, in

Figure 19. Six-bird and four-bird English willow baskets in open position (manufactured by Messrs Sturgess, Leicester).

Figure 20. Twelve-bird double-decked aluminium show container.

Figure 21. European-style show containers in wood and hardboard, double-decked for ten birds.

my view, substantial. They absorb shock and knocks, provide good circulation of air and are free from condensation and the sweating which occurs with metal/plastic containers.

Baskets treated properly will last for decades. They should be scrubbed and varnished regularly and such treatment will be repaid in service lasting for long periods.

Medicine Store

Being a non-medical man, I am always reluctant to advise on the use of medicines for pigeons. There are people qualified to do that. I merely advise all fanciers to have a ready store of a few medicines or treatments which might assist if something goes wrong in the loft. Generally pigeon ailments are the common ones which can be treated with the many preparations on the market. A ready supply may well prevent spread of disease should it strike. Every fancier should also have access to literature on ailments in pigeons, so as to be able to identify anything which occurs. However, if there is the slightest doubt, then expert medical or veterinary advice should be sought at an early stage.

For the showman, however, there might be other items which should be kept in the medicine store. Insect dusting powder, aerosol insecticide sprays, nail-files, nail-clippers, french chalk, sharp scissors, pure soap and tweezers might be included, for often they can be stock-in-trade items. It is always better to be prepared.

Miscellaneous Items

There are many other smaller items which will be necessary for use within the loft. A good scraper is an item which should be in almost daily use. Cleanliness of the loft is so important for show candidates, and the presence of the fancier going about his chores will form part of the management function which allows bird and master to be confident in each other.

For many years, I used sand on the floors of my loft and, from time to time, have tried other materials, such as straw, sawdust, wood chippings and newer materials of a more chemical nature of the type used for cat litter. All have drawbacks, the main one being the dust that is transmitted. Dust of that type, coupled with the natural bloom dust from the pigeons tends to make our hobby somewhat dangerous. All fanciers should have regard to this problem and I would strongly advise the use of a mask (Figure 22) when cleaning the loft and during any prolonged stays there. To be prepared in such a way may ward off respiratory troubles later on. In the past, too little thought has been given to this aspect but the longer I am in the sport, the more worried I become about it.

Figure 22. Rod Wright, Secretary of the National Pigeon Association, wearing a helmet/mask in his loft.

As a result, I firmly believe in clean floors, a factor achieved by the use of the scraper and brush. The floor can then be sprinkled with lime or one of the more modern floor dressings, which not only look and smell pleasantly but also act as insecticide and anti-germ agents.

In this respect, another development has been in the supply to the fancy of all-purpose vacuum cleaners fitted with scraper heads, which will remove all droppings as well as feathers and other dust. These are yet another boon to the fancier's list of accessories.

In dealing with the dust and ventilation problem, one might also have regard to the provision of a form of air extraction – either electrical or a natural air turbine – and during hot weather the employment of an air fan to keep the air constantly on the move and to dispel dust and feather particles.

These and all matters are worth thinking about and I have in this chapter merely attempted to discuss the problems and the possible remedies, as well as the use of both essential equipment and that which might be regarded as a luxury. Shape your loft to your needs and use it as best befits you and your team.

Chapter 4

Entering Shows

In this chapter I would like to say a few words about the procedures involved in entering pigeons for shows. To the experienced showman, a lot of what I am going to say is a matter of course but it does no harm to have a reminder. However, my main intention is to give advice to the novice or the newcomer to showing, so as to make the task a little easier and more understandable.

For those who are unfamiliar with showroom terminology, the various ways of expressing the contents and ideals of the show can be rather confusing and, indeed, misleading. A schedule is the most common method of communicating the necessary information to the would-be exhibitors, although some shows, instead of despatching numerous schedules, use the columns of fancy press magazines to advertise the show and to state the classification and other instructions. The schedule comes in various forms, from the elaborate glossy types used at the classic and national shows to the duplicated sheet of the club and smaller events. Whatever the form, it should contain all the basic information to allow the most novice fancier to be able to enter without serious mistake. A good schedule is precise and free from ambiguity. It follows, therefore, that the best and most informative are those which impart all the necessary information first and then follow with the show regulations.

The exhibitor should always make a detailed study of the schedule (Figure 23) and its contents. It should not be taken for granted that the classification and conditions are the same as for previous years, for more often than not there is some change. Obviously, the date and venue should be first specified to be followed by the classification (Figure 24) together with the names of judges. This should be immediately followed by details of the entry fees, the prize money (if applicable) and details of special prizes and trophies on offer. This basic information should then be followed by the section which deals with instructions, which should cover such details as the closing date for entries, times of penning and the commencement of judging, times of unpenning, when the show opens to the public, and all other show rules and conditions of entry.

These are the matters which often determine whether a show is to be

```
                    DEVON AND CORNWALL SHOW RACER SOCIETY
                            1983/4 SEASON
              * * * * * * * * * * * * * * * * * * * *


SHOW
SATURDAY 17th DECEMBER 1983
AT THE VILLAGE HALL, KENNFORD, EXETER.
Birds to be penned by 1.30 p.m.


JUDGES
C. Clare, Esq.        Classes 1   4   7
F. Matthews, Esq.     Classes 2   5   8
B. Erasmus, Esq.      Classes 3   6   9



CLASSIFICATION
1  Cock Bred Prior to 1982          2  Hen Bred Prior to 1982
3  Cock Bred 1982                   4  Hen Bred 1982
5  Cock Bred 1983                   6  Hen Bred 1983
7  Cock any age thro' bars          8  Hen any age thro' bars
9  Novice Class

N.B.  Novice class is open to fanciers who have not won two firsts
      in open classes in D. & C.S.R.S. Shows.  Once status is lost
      unable to revert back at any time.


ENTRY FEES    Members 20p.          Non-Members 30p.


ENTRIES WITH FEES BY TUESDAY 13th DECEMBER 1983

                  To:  Mr D. G. Gifford
                       29 Hope Close
                       Crossways
                       Dorchester
                       Dorset
                  Tel. Warmwell (0305) 853010
```

Figure 23. Sample small-show schedule.

efficiently run or otherwise and it follows that great care must be taken
to see that all the conditions mentioned can be complied with. It is at
this stage that the exhibitor should ask himself if he is able to comply
with them all because, if not, he may as well forget about entering. For
example, if the birds have to be penned by 8.30 a.m., so that judging
can commence at 9 a.m., it is wrong to ask to be allowed to arrive a
little later as such a request will only cause embarrassment and
difficulty.

```
FANTAILS
JUDGE
Class
57  Fantails White                              Cock          Adult
58     ,,      ,,                               Hen           Adult
59     ,,      ,,                               Cock or Hen   1983
60  Fantails Yellow                             Cock or Hen   Adult
61     ,,      ,,                               Cock or Hen   1983
62  Fantails Black                              Cock or Hen   Adult
63     ,,      ,,                               Cock or Hen   1983
64  Fantails Saddle                             Cock or Hen   Adult
65     ,,      ,,                               Cock or Hen   1983


    FANTAILS
    JUDGE
66  Fantail Blue                                Cock or Hen   Adult
67     ,,      ,,                               Cock or Hen   1983
68  Fantail Silver or Powdered Silver           Cock or Hen   Adult
69     ,,      ,,      ,,      ,,               Cock or Hen   1983
70  Fantail Red                                 Cock or Hen   Adult
71     ,,      ,,                               Cock or Hen   1983
72  Fantail Lace A.C.                           Cock or Hen   Adult
73     ,,      ,,      ,,                       Cock or Hen   1983
74  Fantail Chequer                             Cock or Hen   Adult
75     ,,      ,,                               Cock or Hen   1983
76  Fantail A.O. Colour                         Cock          Adult
77     ,,      ,,      ,,                       Hen           Adult
78     ,,      ,,      ,,                       Cock or Hen   1983


    ANY OTHER VARIETY NOT CLASSIFIED
79  A.O.V.                                      Cock          Adult
80  A.O.V.                                      Hen           Adult
81  A.O.V.                                      Cock          1983
82  A.O.V.                                      Hen           1983
```

Figure 24. Extract from the National Tippler Union of Wales Open Show, Swansea, held in December 1983, showing classes.

If exhibitors all adhered to the show rules, the job of the organisers would be made so much easier and, while that sounds a simple enough observation to make, it is astonishing how many mistakes are made through carelessness or lack of attention to detail. Whilst for the vast majority, shows are social occasions and can be enjoyed not only by the exhibitors but by the spectators, it must be remembered that at every show, whether large or small, there will be one very hardworking figure — that of the secretary. This is the man who has to do the work and the man whose task is a thankless one, for criticisms are many and praise rare. Good secretaries are rare and therefore it is incumbent upon us all to see that his work is minimised by making the job easier and conforming with show regulations.

Having made a study of the schedule and the show classification, the size of the show team to be entered should be considered. Most fanciers will have a fairly good idea of the numbers to be entered but generally two factors seem to determine the team size. For some exhibitors, the size of the team is fixed by habit or cash commitment. It may well be that finance will run to a team of only ten or twelve, bearing in mind not only the cost of entry but the cost of getting the birds to the show. When public transport is to be used, this is indeed a consideration but when travelling with friends the amount of available space may also play an important part in the decision. Another way, where neither of these considerations applies, is to establish just how many birds are available for entry and then to fit the show entry to those available.

Although most of the work can be done indoors, I always think that it is a good and worthwhile exercise to take the classification list along to the loft and to study the birds in line with the classes available. This allows the fancier not only to check the terminology of the class headings but also to fit them to the birds available to him. The fancier with a small team will be able to enter for shows from his own personal knowledge of the birds and possibly without a visit to the loft being necessary. However, the fancier with a large team will probably have to take a journey to the loft to make his examination and to determine which are fittest for the event. For the novice, I would always recommend that the schedule be carefully studied in the loft in order to pick out the best birds to suit the classification.

When showing is being undertaken on a regular basis, it is certainly a good idea to produce a working plan, where all the birds in the loft are listed in one column with details in columns of all the shows intended to be entered. Although I will deal with show condition in Chapter 8, there is little point in entering pigeons week after week for shows because they will soon lose their condition. It may, therefore, be necessary for the show team to be split, so that a smaller, more compact and fitter team is entered for the shows planned. In my opinion, a good show plan is absolutely necessary.

Another factor which will determine the entry is the judge or judges to be employed at the show. Whilst this may not affect the novice for some while, regular exhibitors will know full well which judges they can expect to do a professional job and will thus be able to enter their birds accordingly with every hope of success. This is where the keeping of a full show record comes into its own, for the wise fancier will know not only which pigeons have scored under which judges but also the type of bird that the particular judge seems to prefer. Colour comes into this and also certain fads which judges seem to apply to their judging, e.g. some judges look for faults and discard birds for relatively minor matters while others judge the birds as a whole and count minor faults as a smaller consideration. Much of this will be a personal matter for memory but the wise exhibitor will always keep a record of judges and their likes and dislikes.

In attempting to write about entering pigeon shows, it is, of course, impossible to try to deal with individual classification titles, for these vary tremendously from area to area and most certainly from country to country. Every breed of pigeon will have its own traditions, precedent and expectation and much of this can be learned only by experience. This must always be borne in mind, together with the strict application of the schedule. For example, if a class for flying tipplers specifies 'any other colour', it is pointless entering a light print if this particular colour has already been specified in an earlier class. Likewise, in racing pigeon circles, if the class is for pigeons likely to race and win at a distance of 400 miles, it is pointless entering a show racer because any good judge should be looking for out-and-out racers to fulfil such a task. I quote these as a couple of examples only but it will show that in almost every breed of pigeon throughout the world there will be matters which need to be studied and considered at the planning stage. If there is any doubt whatsoever, the best bet is to ask and, of course, there are always plenty of experienced fanciers around to give the necessary advice.

Having made all the decisions, the time comes for the clerical work to be done and as much care should be put into this as possible. The secretary will appreciate a properly completed entry form (Figure 25) or blank which includes all the details asked for on it and in the schedule. The exhibitor's full name and address, together with telephone number, the correct class numbers, ring or band numbers if required and, of course, the correct entry fee. If the form or blank is lacking in detail it may well lead to non-acceptance or disqualification or entail the secretary having to write or telephone to clarify a point. Any show organiser will confirm the needless work involved in such matters, which is caused mainly through carelessness. The closing date for entry should always be complied with for generally the date quoted is the last convenient working date for the efficiency of the show. It pays to keep a diary of show dates and the dates by which entry, either by mail or by telephone, should be received. Entries by mail are by far the most convenient and practical and less mistakes are made in this way.

BRITISH PIGEON SHOW SOCIETY
ENTRY FORM
CHAMPIONSHIP SHOW at DONCASTER 3/4th DECEMBER 1983

CLASS No	✔ IF TO BE ENTERED IN CHALL. CLASS.	FOR OFFICE USE		CLASS No	✔ IF TO BE ENTERED IN CHALL. CLASS.	FOR OFFICE FOR		CLASS No	✔ IF TO BE ENTERED IN CHALL. CLASS.	FOR OFFICE USE

ENTRIES CANNOT BE ACCEPTED UNLESS ACCOMPANIED BY THE NECESSARY FEES.
PLEASE COMPLETE ENCLOSED ADDRESS LABEL FOR RETURN OF BASKET LABELS.

ENTRY FEE - £1.30 for each entry   Entries will not be accepted
after the 1st November

I declare that the exhibits to be shown by me are my own property
and I agree to abide by the rules of the National Pigeon Association
and of the British Pigeon Show Society.

I enclose;

	Entry Fees at £1.30	
	Subscription or * Donation (£3.00 min.)	
	Catalogue £1.50 (or by post £1.75)	
	Advert for Catalogue	
	Sale Pens	
	TOTAL	

Signed..........................
NAME...................................
BLOCK LETTERS - PLEASE
ADDRESS...............................
....
....
.................Post Code.............

* this is not your
subscription to the
Nat. Pigeon Association

All cheques etc to be made out to the
BRITISH PIGEON SHOW SOCIETY
(43 Kent Road, Pudsey, LS28 9BB.W.Yorks)

FIRST CLASS POSTAGE STAMP APPRECIATED
FOR RETURN OF BASKET LABELS, thank you

Figure 25. Concise and informative entry form for a large show.

Once the entries have been despatched, little else can be done until the show organisers send confirmation that the entries have been accepted and, where applicable, details of pen numbers. This of course will vary from show to show and, obviously, from country to country. Exhibitors should always remember that their show baskets or containers should always be properly and clearly labelled and that the individual compartments for the pigeons should also be properly labelled and should, wherever possible, bear the ring number of the pigeon concerned. This helps not only the exhibitor but also the show organiser should anything go wrong in the absence of the exhibitor.

If I have made this chapter seem a little like a show organiser's lament, it is because I am only too aware of the work involved and how much of it is caused through sheer thoughtlessness. It cannot be stressed enough, however, just how important is the planning for entering shows, for proper care and forethought not only avoids mistakes and unpleasantness at the show but makes for ease of successful and enjoyable showing.

Chapter 5

Attending Shows

A good many years have passed since I attended my first pigeon show and I can honestly say that time has failed to tarnish the pleasure I obtain from attending shows, whether they be big or small. For the majority who keep pigeons for show purposes, going to and attending shows is what the whole business is about and I think it worthy to say a few words on the subject, in order to produce successful showing. Again, as in the last chapter, I am writing mainly for the novice or newcomer and I trust that the more experienced breeder will bear this in mind. The expert who has been attending shows for years will have his own approach and pattern and will not need guidance on this matter.

In attempting to write for the newcomer, I will try to recall my early days and endeavour to re-experience my entry into the sport which has had me firmly dedicated for all these years. In racing-pigeon circles, the thrill of the racing win, the sheer delight of seeing the racer returning to the loft from the race, is the reward, but for the showman the showroom holds the key to all endeavours. The important win is the wonderful experience which makes the hard work, planning and tribulation seem worthwhile, for this is when confirmation is given by one or more judges that one's own judgement and expertise is sound.

My first-ever show was at a small evening-club show where I took along three pigeons, one for myself and one each for two friends to be entered in the class for novices. They were conveyed in a wooden box which I had painstakingly constructed and painted over a period of some weeks and it was a very great thrill when I left that showroom with a red card bearing my name and it was with jaunty pace that I walked the three miles home, bearing my precious load.

Indeed, in my earlier days, my showing was restricted entirely to local-type shows and my attendance was restricted solely to shows within service-bus distance. Other showing was achieved through the use of the railway system which, in those days, was very good, with a reliable service and even delivery to one's home on the return journey. Although nowadays the railway system is rarely used by fanciers to get their birds to and from the shows, my records reveal that, in one year, I sent birds to no less than seventeen shows using the rail system. A lot of my excitement, therefore, came in the parcels office of the nearest railway station when I checked my birds home after a show – an enjoyment more often than not shared with the station staff, who were just as eager as myself to see the results.

My pattern of showing, however, changed after I had attended my first-ever classic show in the early 1960s. With my four entries, I gained a second and a fourth prize in quite large classes and was therefore extremely pleased but it was the whole atmosphere of the show, and the interest of all present, which convinced me that there was far more to showing pigeons than merely at the local level. I realised that the classics were the shows to win, where the real showing was done by the top showmen of the day. I think it is fair to say, without over-dramatising, that my life changed from that time onwards. This, of course, is not unique to me or to anyone taking up pigeons as a sport, but would apply equally to anyone starting a new and all-absorbing hobby, such as golf or angling. I therefore feel that my decision to attend the classic show was the main factor which affected my showing habits and, since then, I have regarded the classics as the main events of my year. In fact, it would be fair to say that my off-duty moments are largely decided in the interests of being able to get to the large shows.

For those with aspirations to win at the sport of pigeon showing, attendance at shows is the best way of gaining experience and expertise, and perhaps the only way in which the seasoned exhibitor will be able to keep abreast of modern needs and changes. The classics are doubly important in this respect, although top-class competition does not only occur at such events, as attendance at any specialist breed show will testify. In general, going to shows is the way in which experience is gained and held and where the enjoyment of the showing side of the sport can be gained. It is a thrill getting the birds back from a show and opening the basket to see whether the birds have gained success, but there is nothing like the thrill of going with the birds and seeing the strength of the competition and whether the judging reflected the quality of what was on show.

The pleasure is in placing into the pens birds which are supremely fit and therefore have every chance of winning and being able to compare favourably with other exhibits. The winning is important, of course, and will add to the pleasure, but the main thing is the enjoyment and the opportunity to observe and plan for improvement. Shows are social occasions and this, within any sport, is a very important part. There are opportunities for fanciers of whatever interest or viewpoint to meet and discuss the sport under relaxing and social conditions. It is the dedicated showman's opportunity to make a thorough study of all the exhibits to see what is doing the winning and why, and who the successful fanciers are. It is most useful to make a study of how a judge has placed the awards and to note the type he has picked and on what apparent basis. I have always kept a record of judges and the type, colour, and other interesting factors of the birds which have won under them. Such a record is a most useful guide when working out the entry to be made at a particular show.

One of the great difficulties in showing today for the novice is the wide variation of judging displayed at the shows and, as a result, winning can often be a hit-and-miss affair, especially in breeds with no written standard. It might be, therefore, that in a show with twenty judges there will often be twenty different types of pigeon winning. Even in breeds with a written and illustrated standard, there are always variations of type and detail. Additionally, judges have fads and fancies which lead them to make decisions in and around the standard. By way of contrast, the winners at a specialist breed show will most certainly be representative of the breed in question because they have not only been shown by people who understand the breed but have been judged by fanciers who either keep the breed or have understanding and sympathy for it. The novice will, therefore, have to make up his own mind as to type, but overall he will gain an opinion based not only on what is winning consistently but on what other fanciers have to say. Around the show hall, there will be a great deal of talk and the novice will have to make up his own mind on what is of value or otherwise but, without doubt, there is a great deal to be learned.

Success in the showing game is hard gained and it takes time and considerable patience, together with more than a measure of luck. It is not often that success comes early in one's career and it is far better and satisfying to work up to success than to start at the top and perhaps work down.

With those few more general observations I will return to the show hall and the general intention of this chapter. When attending shows, the main rule is to arrive in good time so as to give one's stock the maximum possible time to settle. The pre-judging period is a vital one for the exhibitor in adding the final touches to his entry. Such work can only be done if the time of arrival allows for it and there is no need to rush. For local shows it is a good plan to aim to be there at least half an hour before the latest time given in the schedule and with classic shows, where considerable travelling distance is involved, there is need to make a far greater allowance and perhaps the importance of the occasion should be the guide for this. It is important that the birds have time to settle, especially after a long and tiring journey. Some birds are visibly shaken by a journey and take time to recover enough to regain composure in the show pen. By making a study of individual pigeons, it will be possible to see which travel and settle well. The older birds generally need far less time because they have seen and experienced it all before whereas the younger and more inexperienced entries will require the maximum of attention and care at this stage. This is the time when last-minute observation and study can play an important part. It may take time but it will repay tenfold the effort involved.

Each bird should be taken from its show basket or container carefully so as not to ruffle the feathers. It should then be studied for any soiling of the flights, tail feathers and undersides. If the soiling is not too serious, it can be removed with a slightly damp cloth. A check should also be made around the face because birds, through nervousness or other causes, are often sick in transit and there may well be traces of this present which can be removed in the same way. A check should be made to ensure that no feathers have become bent and if any primaries or tail feathers are so found they can be made right by holding them over steam or by applying gentle pressure against the direction of the bend, to allow circulation back into the feather. The feet and legs of the bird should also be checked for dirt and before the bird is placed into the pen (which should be checked to make sure it can be properly secured), a final check should be made on all cover feathers to ensure that none are out of place. Once the bird is in the pen then it should be checked to ensure that its stance is correct and that it looks the part for the judge.

Given the time, another important check which can be made is to arrange the positions of entries in a class according to what else is so entered. In this respect, I am particularly thinking of colour; for instance, if one's entry is a blue bar and it is in the centre of a dozen or so other blue bars its chances can be diminished as a result. The mealy, however, in between dark chequers, might stand out so very much better and catch the judge's eye. I am quite convinced that a bird's position in the class can make a big difference to its chances. Numerous examples could be quoted but just consider a mixed class of jacobins where a white penned in between blacks or reds will certainly stand out. Sensible observation and amendment at this stage of a show can pay dividends and give great pleasure when it pays off by way of success.

When all this necessary work has been done, it may be possible to have a quick look at other entries and to make note of likely opposition. Various methods are used to get birds to settle and perhaps this illustrates the value of pen training pigeons at home prior to shows. Some fanciers use a small quantity of small seed as a means of getting the bird to feel at home in the pen, but this is dangerous for, unless every seed is eaten, the pen could well be deemed a marked one. This maxim applies only where the birds are to be judged in their pens but in some breeds, where the birds are removed to judging pens for judging, then there is less risk. This especially applies in the USA where at the large shows most of the judging is done by the judge sitting in front of large pens into which the birds are placed for his perusal.

In talking about marked pens, it is of great importance also to ensure that the birds are not artificially marked in any way for they are liable to disqualification. Race rings or coloured celluloid rings are sometimes left on by mistake and many judges will refuse to judge such entries. In racing-pigeon classes, wing-stamping presents a more difficult problem and here the only solution seems to be to obliterate the printing so as to avoid any chance of owner-identification.

This just about covers the pre-judging period which, as I state, can be used to great advantage as well as being a period of enjoyment when one can savour the show atmosphere, its competition and excitement. Of course, when the judging commences in Britain the usual rule is that exhibitors are excluded from the hall and, in many ways, I feel this is a great pity for my own experience in judging leads me to believe that it is far more beneficial for the exhibitors to be allowed to stay and to watch the judging to see that all is done fairly. In the USA and other parts of the world, the judging is very much part of the spectators day out for they all sit in rows and watch the judging. This is the main part of the excitement at shows for the exhibitors and I find it difficult to understand why in Britain we do not try this for ourselves. Certainly I believe that it would be useful to see all judging being carried out as it brings matters out into the open and all is seen to be fair. Whatever the system, however, the exhibitor must always observe a strictly neutral position so as to give no hint as to ownership.

The judging completed, the time arrives for the truth to be met and to discover whether all the labour at home and before the show has been worthwhile or in vain. Disappointment is often hard to bear but there is no use in giving vent to anger or frustration at the judge because his decisions are final. It is in order to ask why a particular bird was turned down but do try to do this without lack of grace. Novices can learn a lot from what the judge has to say and I would always encourage an exhibitor to speak with the judge and to seek his advice.

It is rare for the seasoned fancier to question the decisions made for he knows that, in the main, it is a matter merely of preference. However, for the novice and the expert alike, the post-judging period can also be very valuable as a means of learning more about showcraft. It is a most useful exercise to make a study of the winning pigeons and to try to gauge what the judge in question has been looking for. This is the time to make notes for future guidance.

I would stress at this point that offers of help are always appreciated by the secretary or show organisers. There are always plenty of jobs to be done in connection with a show and the more helpers the quicker and easier the tasks become. The work involved in organisation is great and can only be appreciated by those who have done some of it. The quickest way for the novice to learn the trade is to do some work at the shows and to feel for himself just what is involved. By so doing, he will very soon become an accepted part of any organisation if he is recognised as a worker. Such offers will be particularly appreciated at the close of the show when the pens have to be dismantled and carted away and the showroom cleared up. This is the time when all but the most keen disappear and the same old few seem to be left to do the work.

Show regulations are made to be complied with and this is never more apparent than at the time when the basketing procedure begins at the conclusion of the show. The fancier is his own worst enemy for impatience at wanting to get his birds back into the baskets and away. This impatience only makes it easier for theft to take place and it is during the basketing time that thieving of birds occurs. Exhibitors can show their appreciation of show organisers who take the trouble to provide adequate safety measures by keeping to the regulations and ensuring that no bird is removed from the pen except by or in the presence of a steward. It is, therefore, most important to ensure that the colour and ring number of each bird is clearly written on individual compartments in the basket or other show container. In conclusion, I would like to say that whilst shows are wonderful social occasions and are staged to be enjoyed, they need to be worked at by the exhibitor to get the maximum value to prepare him for future events. By all means enjoy the social aspect but novices and newcomers especially should use the opportunity at each and every show to make a study of the winning birds and of the methods of the winner exhibitors. This, after all, is the craft of showmen.

Chapter 6

A Showing Record

A show record is an invaluable accessory to any serious-minded showman. Properly and faithfully completed, it will provide a document of considerable value and lasting pleasure and I seriously recommend any fancier venturing into pigeon showing to keep a full record of events and occurrences both within the loft and at shows.

Such a record should be commenced at the earliest possible stage so that nothing is left to memory and so that the earliest of detail is recorded, to form the basis for future years. It is therefore necessary to give a lot of thought to the form of the record, because not only should it serve in the short term but it should also be capable of expansion to cope with all future requirements.

My own system dates back to the acquisition of my first pigeons and now offers a complete record of all my acquisitions and disposals, breeding details, shows, and details of showing performances of individual pigeons. I have proved to myself on countless occasions just how fickle the memory can be and there is absolutely no substitute for being able to refer to the record to establish any fact required within the loft of pigeons.

When I made my entry into the sport, it occurred to me that I would need a form of record and I intended that it should be mainly for pleasure, adding another benefit to the sport I was enjoying so much. Since then, the value has become much more apparent and the record has become an invaluable aspect of my pigeon fancying.

I therefore gave some thought to what form of record would be best to take me through the years, allowing for expansion and ease of reference. I decided on a 'loose-leaf' form because of its practicality and facility for expansion. I had seen fanciers with ledger-style books which were attractive but lacked the flexibility of the loose-leaf idea and I decided to design my own system around the 'ring-binder'.

Ledgers lack flexibility as when the space for a particular item runs out, as happens, for instance, particularly in the breeding section, then a second ledger may have to be resorted to although the original one may still have plenty of space elsewhere. With a loose-leaf system, however, pages and sections incorporating any later ideas can be added at will.

What I worked out as being my requirements has stood the test of time very well and very few changes have had to be made over the years. I believe that the initial choice of system should be thought out well initially because change at a later date is extremely time-consuming and difficult. One should think about the records which are likely to be required for reference and then shape the system to meet them. Facts should be entered in the record as soon as possible to keep it as accurate as possible. It may be helpful to use a smaller loft book to record details in the loft, all of which should ultimately be transferred to the main record. It is especially important during the breeding season to take details of the dates of laying, hatching and the listing of colours and ring/band numbers. A smaller book might also be reserved for recording details at shows, including names of judges, numbers in each class and so on. Such details can be transferred to the main record at a more convenient time.

The main aim, however, should be to ensure that full information is written in at the earliest possible date. Memory will never cope with the vast amount of information which is amassed over the years and I am always amused at those who fail to keep a record yet boast of wins and other items which could never be established in fact.

My efforts have therefore produced a record which, of course, makes most sense to me, but which hopefully could also be followed by anyone else. The ancestry of all the pigeons in the loft can be traced, thus making the compilation of pedigrees a relatively easy matter – and most certainly accurate. Through the breeding section in particular, I can, in many cases, trace my family of pigeons back to my initial purchases; it is surprising sometimes to look at a pedigree and to find that four generations can take one back 20 years or so.

This underlines the importance of a record in producing a family of birds. This will be mentioned elsewhere (p.60) but it cannot be overemphasised that in formation of a family, the ability to refer constantly to an accurate record is very necessary. I have always valued family progression and feel certain that this applies to any breed of pigeon.

Any newcomer to the sport should soon realise that the blending and maintenance of a true family of pigeons is the surest and best way of producing winning pigeons year after year. The greatest pleasure is in winning with home-bred birds, not those purchased or presented by others. The rewards of producing the winners are enormous in self-satisfaction and sense of achievement.

My record has now spread into a second binder and the chances are that further expansion will be required within a year or so. I therefore now maintain a working binder, containing details of all birds at present with me and this is reasonably compact. The bulk of the record is in the 'dead section' binder, which contains details of all birds no longer with me, breeding details of more than five years ago, and generally all matter which is older in nature and therefore less likely to be required on a day-to-day basis. It seems to work very well and is less cumbersome when kept in this way.

As and when a bird is disposed of, its record is transferred to the second binder and properly indexed. A certain investment by way of time is necessary to keep the system operating but much of the work is done in the evenings by the fireside and it is surprising just how much interest and pleasure can be found within the pages, especially those yellowing slightly with the years!

I would now like to describe my own system in more detail, to present it not as a model, but as a means of giving some idea of the requirements on which individual needs can be based.

(a) Binder I selected a 9×7 inch (23×17.5 centimetre) system because the refills were readily available and because I found it to be a manageable size. This has proved to be the case although thought might be given to having a larger A4-size paper and binder.

(b) Index I always use an index at the front of my current record which I keep reasonably up to date. It is a quick reference when one wishes to look at the details of a particular bird. It lists ring/band number, colour, sex and details of breeder (if other than self). For those with small teams there will be little need for an index but for fanciers with more than a six-pair loft, then I would recommend its use.

(c) Section 1: Individual Pigeon Record This contains a sheet for every pigeon kept in the loft except for young, unshown pigeons. However, as soon as it is decided to keep a young pigeon permanently, either by virtue of breeding potential or show success, a new sheet is entered for it.

The front of the sheet is provided with a number and then shows fairly full details of the pigeon, including colour, full band or ring numbers, sex, details of parentage, together with their respective reference numbers in the system, date of hatching and any other important information (Figure 26). The front sheet is therefore the information sheet and will be added to as time passes. Included here would be any detail such as illness, damage, whether flying out, breeding peculiarities, i.e. slow layer, and indeed anything which affects the performance of the bird in the loft. Also, wherever possible, I include a photograph of the bird and the value of these grows as the years pass.

```
BLUE HEN          'CHAMPION KEMYEL GEM'
NU 74 D 66244
Hatched 1.4.74    Sire  BLUE NU 72 D 69625 (2b)
                  Dam  MEALY NU 72 E 96704 (5e)
Sister to 'No. 49'. Considerable winner for P.J. Kelsey.
Sister to 'Gamble's Blue'. Winner for the late Francis Gamble, inc. 3 X Best
   in Show. Hen now in USA.
'Gem' died 20.3.82 while sitting two eggs. No signs of illness.
```

Figure 26. Section 1: Individual Pigeon Record (Front)

Date	Show	Class Title	Name of Judge	Prize	No. in Class	Winnings
4.10.74	BODMIN	Young hens	S. Guy	–	40	–
17.10.74	DEVORAN	Young hens	W.F.J. Bennett	V.H.C.	17	–
9.11.74	G.Y.A.	Young hens (show)	C. Milnes	–	74	–
16.11.74	MONMOUTH	Young hens (show)	M. Finestone	Reserve	75	–
30.11.74	OLD COMRADES	Y. Hens (Racing)	H. Nicholson	1st	94	£9.50
17. 1.75	DONCASTER	L. Flyer Y.H.	A. Pullman	2nd	81	£4.00
8.11.75	MIDLAND	L. Flyer Ad.H.	R. McCarthy	1st	65	£5.00
		Best Opposite Sex			1400	£5.00

Figure 27. Section 1: Individual Pigeon Record (Reverse)

On the reverse side of the sheet are inserted details of all shows attended by the bird, with spaces for date, title of show, class title, name of judge, position won, number in class and details of any prize money or other prize (Figure 27). As a visual check, I tend to underline in red all prestigious wins, i.e. at classic shows or for best in show and other wins of merit.

The individual records are the main stay of the whole system and give details of the birds at the shows, together with their personal identity particulars in the form of a potted history. The numbering system I used was to number each sheet e.g. one to twenty-five and then to record the birds with a letter of the alphabet in addition. Therefore when (1a) is disposed of, the next bird in that spot in the record will be (1b) and so on. This has presented a few problems and, in time, I might well have to transfer to a straight numbering system.

(d) Section 2: Shows This is the record of all shows entered, providing details of date, title and venue of the show, the number of birds entered together with the costings, i.e. rail or petrol, with details of

anything won by way of money or special prizes (Figure 27).

I enjoy this little record which tells me how my showing habits have changed over the years. In my early days, I showed far more frequently than I do now, entering for any show I heard about. In the early days, I used the railway system frequently and costings certainly reveal how inflation has affected the hobby.

(e) Section 3: Acquisition and Disposal of Birds This section lists all sales and purchases I have ever made. I have kept this record more for a personal reference than for economic necessity. I have always tried to record the dates concerned with the purchase or disposal of birds, adding the name and address of the other fancier concerned.

I include in this details of all gifts, indeed every pigeon which leaves or enters my loft. Birds which are culled are not included in the list, but it may have been useful to have included this at the commencement of the record.

The pages merely record the date of acquisition/disposal, the colour, the band/ring number, the name and address of the fancier concerned and the cost – if applicable.

Figure 28. Section 5: Breeding Record

Parents	Eggs	Hatching	Colours of Y.B.S.	Ring/Band Nos.
PAIR NO. 1/82				
	25.1.82	16.2.82	Blue	E 59703
Blue (17g)	27.1.82	One only		
GB 80 S 94250				
	9.3.83	28.3.83	Dark Chequer	E 59712
Blue Chequer (16f)	11.3.83		Dark Chequer	E 59713
GB 79 D 58569				
PAIR NO. 2/82				
	25.1.82	13.2.82	Dark Chequer	E 59701
Dark Chequer	27.1.82		Light Chequer	E 59702 – To
GB 77 P 18515				A. Werner
	9.3.82	28.3.82	Dark Chequer	E 59710
Blue	11.3.82		Dark Chequer	E 59711
NU 75 K 27233				
PAIR NO. 3/83*				
	26.1.82	} Eggs clear		
Blue	28.1.82			
NU 75 K 27257	10.3.82	29.3.82	Blue	E 59714
	12.3.82	One only		
Blue				
NU 74 D 66244				

*Hen died 20.3.82. Eggs transferred to Pair No. 8/82

(f) *Section 4: Statistical* This page is kept for my personal information only and serves solely as a monitor of success or otherwise.

A line is given to each show entered and the numbers of prizes won listed in columns of prizes, i.e. 1st, 2nds, etc. Thus, at the conclusion of a year, it is a simple matter to add the columns to gauge the degree of success. I also use this section to monitor additional successes, such as best in show and other special awards of merit.

(g) *Section 5: Breeding Section* This is a most important part of the record (Figure 28) and one which will be referred to greatly throughout the years. I use sheets on which spaces are provided for details of the parent birds to be recorded, together with details of their colouring, ring/band numbers and the reference number of each within my system.

I have found this a suitable and simple system over many years. The dates of laying and hatching are shown, together with the details of the young birds reared, including their colour and band/ring details. Further notes can be added as necessary, turning to the reverse of the sheet if necessary. I use a small loft book in conjunction with this section. Another system is to use a breeding card for each nest box, even a card or sheet in diagram form for each breeding compartment, showing each nest box and the pairings, so that details of dates, etc. can be recorded at the time. This is most certainly the best method in large lofts where there are many breeding pairs present.

This, briefly, is the form of my own record and I hope that the details given will provide some basis for planning. Browsing through my record system gives me considerable pleasure and it is astonishing how memories can be stirred of pleasant occasions within this wonderful sport.

With a little time and effort – a few minutes a week perhaps – a substantial and comprehensive document will result which will provide endless pleasure, nostalgia and also the information which is so necessary to maintain a successful team of pigeons.

Chapter 7

Food and Methods of Feeding the Show Team

The feeding of a team of pigeons is one of the most interesting, and time-consuming, parts of the day-to-day management. Over the years, a great deal has been written on the subject, but the vast majority of this material has concerned the feeding of racing pigeons and the particular needs of the sport. However, the one striking feature of all that I have read, is the difference in content, attitude and knowledge of the subject.

My intention is to discuss the subject with show pigeons very much in mind because their requirements are very different to the average racing team. Systems used by racing enthusiasts, however, have much to commend them and a study of the successful ones should always be encouraged. This chapter, therefore, is shaped towards the need of showmen and their birds so as to provoke some thought on the implications.

There is certainly no scientific formula which can be used to achieve condition in pigeons because otherwise it would be a simple matter. There are so many factors which determine the condition of pigeons, besides feeding, that if a most successful system, which was constantly producing results, were to be adopted by another fancier, the chances are that these other factors would counteract the apparent successful feeding method and affect expectations.

Even the very best and most expensive feeding mixtures will not produce show condition and long-gone are the days when I thought that this could be so. Indeed, there are so many other matters which have a bearing on the state of the pigeons and their health. Take, for instance, the loft environment; this must be a settled one for the pigeons to be happy and contented and factors such as the state of ventilation, cleanliness, the time the fancier is able to spend with the birds and the direction in which the loft faces must all be taken into account. Worm infestations, the presence of lice, other illnesses or dietary deficiencies will also affect the condition of the birds and, in such instances, no amount of good food is likely to rectify matters.

Pigeon management is very much an all-round system of work and procedures within the loft, with food and feeding being but one – albeit important – aspect. There are many complications, not least of which, in a general consideration of feeding, are the widely differing needs of the many breeds of pigeons found in shows throughout the world. For example, the dietary requirements for the large breeds, such as the runt or the exhibition homer, will be far different from those of the short-face breeds, although perhaps some of the methods of feeding will pertain to most breeds.

Collective terms are difficult to describe in the feeding of pigeons because terminology varies so greatly between countries. Here in Britain, for instance, 'corn' is a collective term for all types of grain, whereas in the USA, 'corn' refers specifically to maize. Other grains have different titles and even peas, for instance, vary greatly in type and appearance.

I have noticed that, in racing circles, great changes are taking place in attitudes towards the problem of feeding pigeons. The trend seems to be very much on mixtures which have a smaller legume content with more and more of the cereal grains being included. It has always been an accepted fact in Britain that mixtures for racing and showing should contain a large proportion of legumes, mainly in the form of peas, beans and tares. Changes being introduced from Europe, mainly Belgium, mean that mixtures comprise mostly cereals.

In the past, I have referred to mixtures as being light or heavy, depending upon the legume content, and I still feel that these are reasonable terms to use. Certainly the present changes seem to spell out further the wide variations in feeding methods and ideas, as can be seen by a study of various pigeon books.

For show pigeons, I believe that the content of the grain to be fed is less important than the method by which it is fed and all the other considerations of loft management. I have seen condition gained by some fanciers feeding nothing but tic beans, others by a mixture of turkey pellets and wheat, and yet others by a very cheap mixture of cracked maize, barley and wheat of dubious quality.

Above all, we must come to terms with the fact that more often than not our birds are being kept in artificial surroundings by being confined in lofts with no access to the outside world. Also, we must recognise the fact that, however well looked after, our birds will sometimes be better and look better than at others. In nature, wild life has all the advantages and disadvantages of living in its natural surroundings, gaining food from wherever possible and taking other ingredients of life as and when they can.

However bad the Winter, bird life will survive and, despite deprivations, will be fit enough to breed and rear young by the Spring. Our pigeons are confined to the loft and have to make do with what we give them. Many fanciers, especially racing men, encourage their birds to go to the fields to search for their food, grit and other needs but, for the fanciers who live in cities, or who have breeds which cannot have their liberty, this is impossible. Therefore it is important to come up with the right sort of management to suit the team in question, so as to be able to produce that peak of condition as and when required.

Every fancier will therefore have to work at his craft and try to find the vital system which will suit the needs not only of his team of birds, but also the time he has available to spend with them. For this reason, it would be wrong of me or any other writer to state categorically that there is a simple solution. There are certain guidelines which can help but it is mainly a question of the right system for the right loft.

I am continually striving to find better methods of management within my loft as I have already mentioned when talking about pigeon lofts and their construction (Ch. 2). Over the years, therefore, I have changed my methods of feeding considerably and also the type and content of grain. I hope that one day I will come up with the answer on what is best for me, but so far I have been thwarted in no small way by my changes of address and of lofts. However, the more I read, the more I learn, and my chances should be better now having seen the methods and beliefs of so many other fanciers.

I believe that any fancier who finds the successful way of treating his birds should stick to it whatever and be extremely reluctant to change it in any way without good reason. I also feel that all breeds of pigeon, whether large or small, should be treated as the hardy birds which they are and not as delicate creatures. This applies particularly to the fancy breeds, especially those which seem exotic and far-removed from having a flying ability. This is true for almost any form of animal or bird and people would get far more pleasure out of their pets if they were to treat them in a more natural way instead of trying to shield them and protect them from events.

Fancy pigeons of the small type sometimes appear so delicate as to require careful handling but my experience is that the nearer to nature their care can be the better they will respond to management and the better condition will be produced for showing. If birds can be given their freedom to fly so much the better and, where this is not possible, access to a flight or aviary will add a new dimension to their existence. This natural treatment most certainly applies to food and feeding and small birds will cope with normal mixtures if allowed to do so, although obviously allowances will have to be made for the short-face breeds.

The guidelines for grain are really quite straightforward. The best corn available should be purchased and by that I mean not the most expensive, but the best available for the price which can be afforded. I do not intend this to mean only polished grain, because husk and dust does not necessarily signify poor grain. A great deal extra will have to be paid for the polishing when the birds may prefer some of the husk and small seed which often accompanies the main grains.

The best should include only grain which is of good quality, free from mould, dampness, or any contamination. The 'nose' test will always reveal a lot about grains and, if there is the slightest doubt about the freshness, it is best left alone. Likewise, the grains should be hard, especially wheat and barley, as well as the legumes, such as beans, peas and tares. It is very much a matter of experience and newcomers are therefore best advised to go only to reputable dealers or to seek other advice before they gain the necessary skills to judge for themselves.

Peas and beans, in particular, should be uniform in size and appearance with no signs of shrivelling. Always check that grain is free from weevils, evidenced by holes in the grains. Samples of peas or beans with some black or blue/purple ones will most certainly indicate that they have been exposed to damp or have not been dried properly and they should be discarded. Wheat and barley should be plump with no signs of fungus markings. Corn or maize should be free from signs of mould or discolouration.

Care should be taken over the feeding of new season's grains because they can be extremely upsetting to the digestion if fed when too fresh. It is far better to store it for a while, but if circumstances enforce its use, it is better to introduce it gradually by mixing it in increasing portions with existing feeds. This applies to any changes in diet which should always be made as gradually as possible and never by a sudden and complete change.

The actual seeds to be given will vary from loft to loft and even from breed to breed. There is no question, therefore, of suggestions as to mixture contents being recommended here. Suffice to say, however, that over the year, I much prefer to feed a mixture which varies from season to season. For the breeding season, I like to use a wide selection of grains, including a proportion of pellet feed and supplements containing mineral and vitamin additives. Usually this will include a fair amount of beans and peas, making it a fairly heavy mixture.

I continue to feed the same sort of mixture through the period of the moult, to ensure that the birds have plenty of variety during this stressful time. I simply believe that the wider the selection of grains the better the chances of the birds getting their full nutritional requirements through the moult.

During the moult, the mixture contains only a reasonable proportion of legumes but I tend to increase this proportion as the show season approaches. In other words, I make the mixture a fairly heavy one by using more beans and peas but no pellet feed. At the conclusion of the show season, and in the period prior to the breeding programme, the mixture is made considerably lighter, especially with the addition of barley in high proportion; this reduces fat and equips the hens in particular to lay without unnecessary stress. The mixture is then enriched during incubation so that the birds are at their best by time the eggs hatch.

This is a rough outline of what I administer to my birds but there are always adjustments to cater for weather conditions and for other occurrences within the loft, especially immediately prior to and immediately after shows. It is all non-scientific but I believe that experience in the actual feeding is the best and only real guide.

Whether my mixture is light or heavy therefore depends upon the time of the year. It is also important to have some knowledge of the constituents of the grains used and their effects on the body. In the very broadest of terms, the following applies: the protein enables the muscles, skin, bone, feathers and other tissues to grow; the carbohydrates are the elements which keep the body warm and supply its energy; fats and oil function in the same way as carbohydrate. The other constituents are mineral salts, vitamins and, of course, water. Each of these six constituents should be present in the daily diet of the pigeon.

With this in mind, the following table lists the various properties of the main grains fed nowadays. It must be remembered that all percentages are approximate and will vary with almost every sample depending upon its overall quality.

Comparative Table of Grain Consituents

Grain	Protein %	Carbohydrates %	Fat %	Fibre %
Maize	7.1	65.7	3.9	2.2
Wheat	11.3	64.0	1.2	1.6
Barley	9.3	62.2	1.2	4.5
Tic Beans	20.1	44.1	1.2	7.1
Maple Peas	19.4	49.9	1.0	5.4
Kaffir	7.7	60.5	3.0	1.9
Buckwheat	8.5	42.3	1.9	14.4
Vetches (Tares)	22.9	45.8	1.5	6.0
Sunflower	14.6	10.3	30.7	28.1
Hemp	13.7	16.8	29.3	15.0
Safflower	16.3	29.8	29.5	26.6

The one factor not previously mentioned but included in the table, is the fibre content. It is felt by many that the fibre content should be fairly high and can be compared to more modern thinking on the need for additional fibre intake by human beings. It will be seen that barley, beans, peas, buckwheat, tares, sunflower, hemp and safflower have the greatest percentage of this and they should figure highly in any proposed mixtures.

All in all, I regard the mixtures as having the best possible ingredients for our pigeons. I know of fanciers who feed only tic beans and swear that this gives their pigeons hard, compact body weight, but I am still inclined to the opinion that this is more a result of a suitable environment than this rather monotonous diet. We all like variety in our diet and prefer a change. The same must apply to our pigeons and we are all aware of the preferences of our birds for certain grains. Pigeons have a sense of taste and greedily eat some grains at the expense of others, generally disliking seeds with a pronounced hull or husk such as sunflower or oats, yet loving hemp and safflower.

The content of mixtures can therefore differ greatly and will depend to a large extent upon the availability of grains to the fancier. Tic beans are plentiful in Britain but comparatively rare in the USA, although the reverse applies to kaffir, milo and safflower. The best available locally will therefore be the important consideration. It will therefore be for the fancier to estabish his own mixture with availability and need in mind as well as other factors such as the environment.

From the mixture we can now turn our attention to the method of feeding for I regard this as being equal in importance to the content of the feed. This is where management takes over, prescribing habit within the loft and the strict attention to detail to suit the team in question.

The method of feeding is very important and on it can depend to a great extent the success or otherwise of the show team. Generally, the two methods used are hand-feeding or feeding by hopper, sometimes referred to as self-service. Each has advantages and disadvantages, and here again the fancier will make the choice not only according to the inmates of his loft, but to his own commitments and time available to spend in the loft.

Hand-feeding (Figure 29) is probably the best method for ultimate management. It depends however a great deal upon the fancier having sufficient time to devote to the system which can be extremely time-consuming. It is probably most suited to the fancier with a small team of pigeons or with a small loft, or, perhaps, the fancier who has plenty of time on his hands, owing to retirement or an occupation which allows him plenty of time for access to the loft and birds.

This system allows the fancier the maximum contact with his birds and should be conducted in such a way as to further this relationship. The hand-feeding may be achieved by distributing the grain onto the loft floor, or onto specially designed and maintained trays. Whatever

Figure 29. *The author hand-feeding his birds.*

Figure 30. Tray-feeding.

method is used, the birds cannot feed unless they approach the fancier and thereby a mutual understanding and trust is built up. The aim should be to allow the birds to feed readily without fear of the fancier but without allowing the grain to become soiled – especially when in contact with the floor.

Trays (Figure 30) are ideal, providing that they are kept clean and free from droppings. The whole system can become a 'play' session where the fancier signals in some way that food is available, such as by producing a tray, either on the floor or hinged so that it is at convenience level, or by some other signal such as a whistle, which the birds will soon understand as being the indication that food is available. Such methods of hand-feeding can be conducted to the discretion of the fancier once or twice a day, or whenever the fancier feels. It is a wonderful way of building up the vital understanding which will contribute to the well-being of the birds.

Hand-feeding helps to keep the birds alert and on their toes, ready and waiting for their food. Slight underfeeding at a session will heighten the desire at future sessions, and this will probably lead to an overall sharpness and intensity in the birds in the loft.

The disadvantages also manifest themselves. There is always the problem of knowing when a bird has eaten sufficiently. The usual guide is that when the first two or three have taken a drink, then the main bulk of the birds have eaten enough. It is just another way of

Figure 31. Pigeons being hopper-fed, the most common system.

keeping them alert. The other problem is that hand-feeding takes a considerable amount of time, especially where there are three or more compartments in the loft. The time required is considerable and feeding must be on a regular basis and, wherever possible, at set times during the day. The final most obvious problem is during the breeding season, when there is probably most need for a regular source of food for the rearing parents. Hungry parents will leave the nest at the signal for food and will know that they have to eat as much as possible because the next feed is probably a long time off. They, therefore, tend to leave the eggs and young birds for longer periods than might be desirable, resulting in chills and possible death to the young pigeons.

Hopper-feeding (Figure 31) does away with fears of this problem but, in turn, produces others. For the fancier with limited time and, for those whose habits are more unusual and subject to other outside influences, hopper-feeding in entirety or in a modified form may be the only answer. The advantages are that there is a constant source of food, removing any anxiety which might exist in the birds, and allowing the birds to take as much food as and when they require it. The advantage during the breeding season is obvious.

The system allows the fancier to plan his own movements and to accommodate the loft and birds in line with his convenience. The disadvantages however are also fairly obvious and are why I usually prefer a modified form of hopper-feeding. With a mixture being used in

69

the hoppers (which should always be covered to prevent contamination), it is obvious that certain grain will be preferred to others and the likelihood is that the most unpopular will be left in the hopper or spread about the floor, having been rejected by the feeding birds. Vermin might then be attracted, or the grains rejected or soiled. Also some birds are liable to overeat and get fat whereas others, lacking the alertness of the hand-fed birds, may lose weight, becoming listless as a result and less likely to feed.

To get round these problems, the fancier may well have to modify his hopper-feeding arrangements so that the hopper may be filled with an appropriate amount in the morning and not replenished until every grain has been eaten. Then, in the evening, following the replenishment of the hopper and after the birds have eaten, the hopper and contents are removed until morning. This removes most of the wastage and still gives the birds reasonable times between meals. For the man with limited time at his disposal, this modified hopper-feeding system may be the best for general management.

Each system has much to commend it but, in general, the ability of fanciers to hand-feed must have considerable advantages to overall management. The better the understanding between fancier and pigeons, the better the chances are of completely calm surroundings being achieved. The combination of hand- and hopper-feeding enables food to be moderated according to the needs of the team. In this way, the best of condition for the best of the pigeons will be achieved.

Whatever the system adopted, it will not be enough on its own. Apart from the birds needing as much sunshine as they can get, they will need a constant supply of grit and, especially during the breeding season, a form of mineral supplement. These will be available at all good pigeon suppliers and should never be forgotten. For birds who are not able to have their liberty a source of greenstuff, such as lettuce or cabbage, is especially important. Birds able to pick around the garden will find most of what they need, but those confined to the loft will need the extra supply. Extra supplements should be given during the rearing season, with additions of calcium and other vitamins.

Without a doubt, a supply of good clean water will have a good deal to do with the condition of the pigeons kept in any loft. The vessels should be clean − that goes without question − and the water should be changed regularly, at least every day and more often where time allows. The market is just about swamped nowadays with potions, medicines and other alleged wonderful substances which can be added to the drinking water to combat illnesses or to aid condition. Most of these are costly versions of day-to-day medicines, such as iron tonics. There is nothing magic about any of those on offer and they should be treated with financial suspicion. They are unlikely to do harm, however, and may very much assist birds, especially at times of stress such as during the breeding season, the moult or before and after shows. Bear in mind the expense and remember that there is nothing magical in them, then treat them accordingly. Some fanciers take the claims too seriously and I often feel that a drinker of good clear water is the best the pigeon can have.

Feeding show pigeons is not always a matter of routine because the aim is always have the team at its best on the day of the show. The first object is to bring the bird to its peak of condition in time for the show and, as described in Chapter 8, there is then the need to get the bird over the trauma of the show and ready for the next outing. The same routine seems to apply to the showman as to the racing enthusiast, and you will quickly learn how to regulate the supply of food so as to reduce condition temporarily and then to build it up again as quickly as possible in time for a planned event or outing.

Hence, a bird having been conditioned expertly for a show will attend the show and probably, as a result, lose some of its bloom owing to the stress of the journey and the mere experience of being subjected to such unreal surroundings.

It will be delighted to return to its loft and will quickly settle back into a routine, providing that allowances are made for it, especially in the supply of food. On its return, it should be given a light feed of its usual diet, to make it feel at home and to settle it. Following this period of re-adjustment, the food supplied may well be reduced for a day or so, resulting in a lowering of condition and possible loss of weight. This may be achieved by a general reduction in amount or by supplying a less liked food, such as barley. After this adjustment in food content for a day or so, the full diet can then be resumed, resulting in a fast return to normal weight and the production of the bloom associated with ultimate condition.

In the main, such adjustments will take somewhat in excess of a week and can best be applied where shows are at least two weeks apart so as to provide the flexibility for the fancier and his management. It is best applied to those breeds judged on handling properties which have a tendency to carry weight. The keener the pigeons are for their food, the better the chances of weight being produced and also better condition.

It is all a fascinating problem and one which requires a great deal of study and experiment in order to find the system best suited to the needs of any team of pigeons – and, of course, the fancier. If the solution is found the result is pleasure gained from the production of sound, healthy and winning pigeons from a minimum of effort in management.

Chapter 8

Show Condition: General Management

This chapter deals with the process of preparing a bird from its loft for its entry into the show pen. It is an art to be able to take birds from the loft in such a peak of condition, that by the application of finishing touches, they are ready for judging, and in with a chance for the honours. A champion pigeon out of condition is reduced to being an ordinary bird and highlights the vast difference between normal fitness and the extra sparkle of super health so necessary for successful showing. It is that sparkle, that extra something, which makes so much difference to the good judge. This chapter therefore is a guide – and no more than a guide – to the production of good condition for showing. Basic management counts for all breeds of pigeons but I would say that it applies even more to those breeds where handling counts so much in the overall result and, by this, I refer particularly to show racers and to the flying breeds of fancy pigeons. In these breeds, of course, not only does the bird have to look its sparkling best but it has to handle correctly, not only in its natural balance but with a suitable body weight to complement it. Fanciers of long standing know, and novice fanciers will soon realise, that certain pigeons seem able to maintain and produce this quality of condition much more readily than others and it is these birds around which any breeding programme should be directed (see Chapter 10).

General management and the production of show condition is an all-year campaign and one requiring a concentration of thought throughout each and every day of the year. In most cases, one gets out of a sport as much as one is prepared to put into it and this undoubtedly applies to the successful keeping of pigeons because there is no substitute for time spent in the loft and the time to think and study the subject at hand. In considering this matter, the whole process can be divided conveniently into five stages.

Management in the Loft
The secret of any successful showman lies in his management within the loft. This skill is required for any form of livestock exhibition or performance competition and the successful person is the one who has

succeeded with his management. Sound and correct management is occasionally both recognised and valued, but often the success is taken for granted, without the fancier knowing exactly what is bringing about the production of good condition. The most palatial loft may be totally unsuitable for its purpose whereas a modest backyard construction, whilst not being pleasing to the eye, may be the exact design for the production of a settled environment. This is dealt with in more detail in the discussion of lofts for showmen (Chapter 2) but my experience leads me to believe that the construction of the loft can have very much to do with the success of the inmates. It is the age-old question of whether it is the fancier or the building contributing most to success and I feel that, in many ways, it is almost better not to find out because, if one has achieved success under certain conditions, then it is generally advisable not to change either the building or working conditions dramatically. All too often, I have seen fanciers change from their modest little lofts to something far more prestigious only to lose the train of success or, indeed, having to work doubly hard to find it again.

Whatever the building or whatever the team, the finest ingredient one can apply to them is that of time. Time will always be repaid by the birds as they become tame and quiet and used to one's presence in the loft. There is little worse than entering the loft to find wild on-edge pigeons; this is a state of affairs which every fancier should avoid because, with such wildness, one's chances of producing peak condition are considerably reduced. The fancier should try to adopt habits not only of regular feeding etc., but also of steady movement so that the birds are rarely if ever surprised by what he does. This is where the novice can gain much by examining the behaviour of the successful fancier within his loft for everything will be done with deliberation in a slow, even, ponderous manner so that the birds feel completely at ease in his presence. This is part of the ingredient of that settled environment.

Another important factor is the number of pigeons kept within the loft. There is no hope of achieving good show condition if birds have to fight for their perches and the aim should always be to have as much space as possible for each pigeon, possibly with two perches available for every one inmate. With pigeons constantly battling for perching space what hope ever is there of them being settled in their loft situation? I have often said that the empty perch is more valuable than its likely occupant and I feel this very strongly because many of the faults found in management are due to overcrowding.

Settled conditions are really achieved by making the loft inmates happy through the fancier's ability to have his birds settled and contented with an apparent enjoyment of life. Birds which fly out are often fitter and more alert than prisoners and breeds which are incapable of flying appreciate access to a flight or aviary where they can sun themselves.

The general guidelines are simple ones and I have often described them as the five rules of cleanliness. These are:

(a) Clean Air There must be a constant supply of clean air within the loft effected by a ventilation system which allows free circulation without a cutting draught. The loft should seem fresh at all times with no apparent odour.

(b) Clean Food The supply of a good quality clean food is very important indeed and perhaps just as important as the method of feeding. All receptacles, trays, etc. should be kept clean so as to allow the food to remain in good condition until eaten.

(c) Clean Water There should be a constant supply of fresh water presented in clean receptacles. Many fanciers use water-purifying tablets to ensure that no germs or contamination are carried in the drinking water.

(d) Clean Loft This involves not only regularly scraping and cleaning the loft to prevent droppings building up but also extends to the washing and disinfecting of the walls and perches. This does not have to be taken too far but time spent in washing the walls is repaid in having a pleasant-looking and clean loft at most times. A suitable spray apparatus is almost a must for every pigeon fancier, not only to disinfect the loft but also, by regular use, to rid it of insect life – mite, etc. The cleanliness of the loft also extends to making it mothproof, particularly during warm periods, for moths seem to hide in the most unlikely places and at night feed on pigeon feather.

(e) Clean Pigeons These are birds which are subjected to regular baths and which are free of insect life, owing to the fancier either regularly spraying or powdering the birds or the loft in general. Cleanliness of pigeons should also be extended to include a regular preventive treatment for canker and worm infestation.

Those are the general guidelines and it is then up to the individual fancier to blend his particular form of management to it. Tonics, potions and other fads are all used and tried and, indeed, the dealers are stocked full with apparently magical supplies which can produce super-pigeons from ordinary ones. Each novice will have to find this out for himself as he proceeds in the sport but his success is likely to be far more permanent if he first keeps to the basics and adds the finishing touches as he proceeds.

Training

The next stage is the intermediate one between the loft management and the actual preparation for the show. It is the period of consolidating what has been done within the loft as a means of preparation for the show. It is a time for training for both the birds and the fancier, who must prepare himself as well as his team.

Training is most important for the birds to ensure that they are accustomed to both the show pen and the show container. Pen training is self-explanatory in that most successful showmen will acquire for themselves a few show pens so that they can regularly get their birds conditioned to being placed into pens and handled accordingly. This, of course, applies especially to young birds for, in general, the older pigeons soon get used to the situation. Pen training certainly makes the trauma of the first show far more bearable for birds and the same applies to being made aware of the show container or basket. It is a fairly simple matter for the basket to be taken to the loft and the birds to be placed in it and removed elsewhere for an hour or so before they are eventually taken back to the loft, removed and replaced in their normal environment.

Whilst talking about show containers, this is the time when the fancier should be getting them ready by ensuring that they are clean and ready for use. Show containers should be scrubbed out in a mild disinfectant solution and baskets should be regularly varnished. In my own case I scrub every year and varnish every 2 years. Such regular attention will rid them of moth, mice and general dirt and it is a fact that a clean well-presented container represents the fancier just as much as the birds he exhibits.

This is the planning period for the fancier, during which time he has to consider the shows he wishes to attend, his method of travel and the space available to him. With these considerations in mind, he will have to consider the size of his team for each of the planned shows and whether there is a need to split the team to be able to cater for the shows. Indeed, the production of a show programme involves as much care as any top racing enthusiast would apply in the production of a race programme so as to ensure that his best candidates are available for the most prestigious races. It requires a great deal of thought and concentration and consideration has to be given to the birds and any likely over-showing. At least two weeks should be allowed between shows and, with this in mind, the fancier will have to consider how to arrange his team.

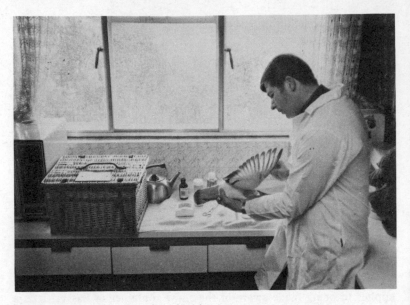

Figure 32. The author preparing a bird for show — making the final checks.

Pre-show Period

This is the period between the making of the entry and the physical preparation (Figure 32) for taking the birds to the show. The fancier will now look at his birds in minor detail and consider whether there is need of feather-trimming or pulling with a view to making his bird comply with the standard, if there is one. He will need to have particular regard to the regulations of his breed to ensure that he does not overstep them and leave himself open to disqualification. Show ploys are somewhat emotive to some and include not only feather-trimming and pulling but darkening of beaks, clipping or filing of the beak, filing of the wattle using a nail-file and trimming of toe nails. All such matters have to be considered in the light of breed regulation.

The basketing procedure time is, of course, most important and, again, time is the key. Fanciers should ensure that the containers to be used are clean and charged with sawdust or wood chippings, straw or other suitable material. They should also be dried and fully aired. The requirements at basketing time are a supply of warm soapy water, a nail-brush and suitable towels, together with chalk or talcum powder to ensure that one's hands are always dry before handling the birds (Figure 33). Chalk in block form may also be kept for whitening the wattle, particularly where there are peck marks apparent and visible. A steam kettle is also useful at this time to cope with bent flights.

A thorough and painstaking look must be taken at each pigeon in

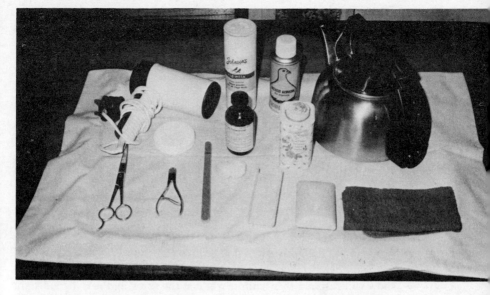

Figure 33. Equipment used in preparing birds for show (from left to right): hair-dryer for drying washed or cleaned feathers; insect powder; insecticide spray; kettle for steaming feathers; French chalk block for whitening wattles; cleaning spirit (carbon tetrachloride) for removal of stains; talcum powder for drying and cleaning hands; sharp scissors for feather trimming; nail-clippers for toe-nails; emery board for sanding over-long growths of beak; cotton wool for use with cleaning fluid; scrubbing brush for cleaning feet and wings; soap; towel for drying hands.

turn; any apparent faults should be noted, and rectified if at all possible. Great care should be taken in handling so as not to disturb or frighten the bird or to interfere with its natural bloom.

Occasionally, birds which are badly soiled may have to be given an individual bath using warm water and a soft or natural form of soap. The soiling should be carefully washed out and then thoroughly rinsed away so that there is no suggestion of staining afterwards. The bird can then be allowed to dry naturally in a warm place or by the use of a hairdryer — it is amazing just how well the feathers dry and resume their natural appearance.

With all the checks complete, the birds should be placed in a warm place before travel and, without doubt, the warmth does tend to draw out bloom from the pigeons, adding to their overall chances. When baskets are used, fanciers often cover the internal compartments with newspaper or brown paper so as to conserve the heat. It is, again, all a matter of personal preference and each fancier will adopt his own particular way of doing things but a painstaking check at this stage will be made worthwhile at the show.

Show Period

It may seem doubtful that anything can be done while the birds are at the show to ensure future show condition but I believe this to be so. If one is not attending the show (perhaps the birds have been taken by a friend), then there is little one can do to those birds but, at home, preparation should be made for their return. This includes not only the cleansing of the loft but also in giving the birds left at home a bath so that, when the show candidates arrive back, they can be also given a bath and will then have it very much to themselves.

If, however, the fancier attends the show there are small matters he can and should attend to, particularly after judging. He should ensure that every bird has been given food and water and, indeed, many fanciers go to the trouble to carry supplies to ensure that their birds are given the same food and water that they receive at home. Some attention to the birds at the show will pay off.

A study of the birds entered at a show can be used as an extension of pen training. Pigeons which have been properly trained prior to the show will respond to attention while at the show and it is a good sight to see tame pigeons in the pen willing to react to their owners. Indeed, birds which are so tame will often attract the eye of the judges, who generally favour tame birds and dislike those who are wild in any way.

Some attention to the birds entered will assist, especially if tit-bits of food are offered so as to make the show outing as pleasant and relaxing as possible for the bird. These are small matters requiring time, but I would assert that it is time well spent and will be repaid in future preparations.

Post-show Period

In my view, this is the most underestimated period in the showman's timetable for it is in the period following the show that the work commences for the next outing. Birds attending a show get very tired and on edge and need a quiet period for recovery. The show pigeon uses energy because it is in a most unfamiliar environment while out of its loft and, like a pigeon returning from a long or tiring race, it also needs time to recover its lost energy. I often quote the example of my wife's dogs: whilst they appear to enjoy an outing to a show, they spend most of the following day sleeping as it seems that far more is taken out of them than appearances suggest.

Although the pigeon needs rest following a show, it can quickly recover psychologically if it is able to fly out. It can achieve its health and fitness, providing that weather conditions allow for liberation. It is always pleasant to see birds when they are returned to the loft from their show containers indicating their pleasure at being home and there is generally a great deal of commotion as a result. However, wherever possible, the bird should be returned to its own particular perch and not allowed to fly from the show container to the perch as this will encourage it to try to escape from the show container, with possible disastrous results at shows.

A light feed is advisable upon return and it also helps if sugar or glucose has been added to the drinking water so as to quickly restore some of the lost energy. Over the years, I have always made it a habit that, at whatever time of the day or night I return from a show, the birds are placed back into the loft so as to reduce as much as possible the actual time spent in the show containers. I feel that this is especially important when returning at night so that the bird awakens the following morning in its familiar surroundings. I cannot overstress the importance of care during the period in question and I strongly recommend that thought be given to it because the quest for show condition begins here.

Chapter 9

Selection of Breeding Pairs

No decisions taken within the loft are more important than those which determine the breeding pairs, for on such decisions will depend the future success or otherwise of the show team. Great thought and care has to be devoted to the subject and it is very much a year-round process based upon observation, experience, knowledge and perhaps a sixth sense. Most fanciers will produce some good youngsters, but the successful ones manage to breed good pigeons year after year.

The considerations to be applied to the show loft are far removed from those required in the production of a team of pigeons for performance, i.e. racing pigeons or competitive flying breeds, such as the rollers and tipplers. Appearance and handling properties are the main matters to be borne in mind whereas, with the performing breeds, stamina, speed, agility and strength are foremost in the minds of fanciers when planning the breeding lists.

What, however, of the breeds which carry some of the responsibilities and needs of both sides of the sport, such as the show racers and the exhibition versions of the performing breeds? For them, not only is the ability to perform important but it is also necessary that they look and handle well enough to satisfy the judges at the shows. The true dual-purpose pigeon is an attractive proposition, with comparisons in the dog world — breeds such as spaniels, labradors and greyhounds being the most obvious examples. Dual champions are rare, whether among dogs or pigeons, but there is great attraction in the thought and many fanciers aim to produce birds capable of such performances.

The purpose of this chapter is to present some observations on the process of producing breeding pairs, not as a guide which can be faithfully followed to produce super-breeders, but as a means of giving food for thought on this most important subject. To simplify matters, I will direct my thoughts to the needs of the average show enthusiast who wishes to produce pigeons of sufficient quality to fit as closely as possible the standard of perfection laid down for any particular breed. Hopefully, therefore, the advice will apply equally to the show racer or flying breed as to the many breeds of fancy and rare varieties that exist, ranging from the simple hardy ones to the more rare and exotic breeds.

The selection of the breeders for the breeding season should never be a lottery and neither should it be done without a great deal of thought and planning. I often think that it is a matter for consideration all the year round, commencing at the conclusion of the breeding season, with the results evidenced in the quality of the youngsters produced, and thought being given towards the aims and hopes of the breeding programme to come.

One is bound to mention the standard pertaining to any breed under consideration. Most breeds of fancy pigeon have a set standard, either written or accepted by precedent, and therefore the application of the standard will be the most important basis for decision because of the necessity to produce pigeons which closely resemble that requirement. In the flying breeds, where there is no written standard, the need is to produce birds which not only look well but have the balance and poise which is so necessary as much of the judging depends on these factors. Whatever the case, it is the fancier's judgement in the end which will lead to the selection of the breeding pairs, with the standard or otherwise being but a pointer towards that judgement.

All fanciers will have set firmly in their minds their ideal pigeon, based upon what they strive to produce annually, or perhaps even birds from the past, and upon birds which have won considerably or which have been accepted or admired for being good examples of their breed. This ideal pigeon must be remembered at all times for only then will it produce the thought necessary to produce it from within the loft and its existing inmates, or by using a bird acquired from outside. What I am saying, therefore, is that such planning should be made throughout the year, with possible pairings being considered based upon the features already mentioned.

Yet another factor also comes into the reckoning – that of pedigree. I have elsewhere in this book expressed the need for the accurate keeping of records and, in the planning stages leading to pairing, the record and the pedigrees formed as a result can be very important indeed. Good show pigeons may have to be thought of in terms of pedigree so that a search can be made in that pedigree to establish other possible combinations to produce the like, something near it or indeed something better. This is what it is all about – the production of a pigeon which is better than its parents or ancestors, something which will suit most judges and keep the bird winning at the shows.

I am confident that, in most lofts, there are pigeons which are consistent breeders of above-average-quality birds. These are to be valued. However, much of the skill here is in identifying, at as early a stage as possible, the value of such pigeons, for they can found a successful loft. It is a mistake to dispose of adult pigeons too soon after breeding has finished. Otherwise, if the quality of youngsters produced is realised too late, there will be no prospect of repeating the pairing. It is always tempting to reduce numbers as soon as possible but the danger of this happening is always there.

Having mentioned the pedigree and its value in either tracing back possibilities as to the reasons for the production of successful birds or searching for likely combinations to produce such birds, I can turn to another important matter – whether to adhere to a set pattern of pairings. In this connection I shall refer mainly to the most accepted methods:

(a) In-breeding is a method of pairing closely related pigeons, such as father to daughter, mother to son, so as to be reasonably certain of producing birds of similar quality. This system tends to 'set' quality with a reasonable expectation – barring freak production of wasters – that the birds produced will be of equal quality to the parents. It is a way of producing a family of pigeons in a short period of time, although it must be remembered that, when this method is used, it is unlikely to yield birds greatly superior to the parents. The favourite expression on this point is that 'a barrel can yield only what it contains' and by such close pairings, the quality is virtually decided. The danger is one of producing weaknesses, faults and lack of virility and stamina. In-breeding should not be attempted by the novice fancier. Considerable experience is required in judging the possible outcome of such a practice.

(b) Line-breeding is a similar system where the pairings are mostly along a family pattern but not so close. This is probably the best and safest method of producing a sound healthy family pattern. It is more like pairing nephews to nieces and cousins to cousins, and so on, keeping a generation between the birds to be paired. I always describe it as being a system of breeding in and around a family pattern, thus ensuring that the birds produced have sufficient outcrossing but are bred close enough to ensure the continuation of the family pattern.

(c) Cross-breeding On the other hand, this method includes pairing together birds from entirely different backgrounds, often more in hope than anything else that good quality birds will be produced. However, that is an extreme description because, of course, the introduction of a cross can be made within a family pattern, increasing vigour and the possibility of enhancing the quality already there.

These are probably over-simplifications of the terms but, as many novices will be reading the chapter, I consider it apt enough for fanciers to get the broadest of ideas. At a guess, I would say that the majority of pigeon fanciers in the showing world will use a system of line-breeding more than anything else because they will realise the value of a family of pigeons. I am adamant that the best chance of success in pigeondom, is for the fancier to produce an exclusive family, not only from the purest motive of self-satisfaction but also from the point of view of ease in consistently producing quality pigeons. I have always fervently believed in the desirability of producing such pigeon families and the best and most successful showmen are those with such related teams. I keep fairly rigidly to a family, although I introduce crosses fairly regularly and, when doing this, would much rather have access to birds from a fancier with a similar set family so that the bird so acquired is far more likely to blend in.

Throughout the year, therefore, thoughts should be directed to the approaching breeding programme with pedigree, past performance and future requirements determining the breeding team. Indeed, the breeders may be separated from the show team. Some of the best may not produce, whereas others, either as stock birds or as birds of promise through their parentage, whilst not being members of the show team, may be allocated specifically to the breeding programme. Of course, numbers will be important because too many pigeons will lead to overcrowding and even more difficulty in pairing the birds. Therefore culling will have to go hand in hand with thoughts of how to pair the birds together.

Perhaps, one day, the ingenious fancier will determine his pairings by computer and such a radical idea would be viewed with interest. The value of the pedigree could then be tested once and for all. However, for most of us, it is a paper exercise with lists of cocks and hens and their likely pairings being depicted according to their relationship, either by blood or likely quality.

I am bound to admit, however, that for many, although pedigree counts for a great deal, it is very much an inbuilt skill that leads to the eventual selection of the breeding pairs. There are fanciers who are fairly successful, who buy and sell consistently and therefore forfeit claims to building their own family, yet year after year manage to produce wonderful youngsters. What is it therefore that allows them to do this, whereas many who stick to the line or family pattern, seem to have to struggle for the few good youngsters they produce? You can tell how successful a fancier is by the quality of youngsters he produces. This has always been true.

It is the art of looking at pigeons and being able to distinguish between those which have breeding capacity for quality and those which have not. It is the skill all fanciers would like to possess but few do.

There are many factors to be assessed when trying to sort out the breeding pairs. Naturally much depends upon the demands of particular breeds and their standards and whether the birds are handled during judging. However, there are some matters which are common and which I will mention as a guide. For instance, there is little worse than to have pigeons which are wild in the loft or in the show pen. Such nervous birds upset the remainder of the loft inmates and stand little chance when being judged. It is uncommon for such birds to be tamed and, often, the only way around the problem is to dispose of them, even though they are excellent show standard candidates. I feel that it is important to breed calmness into one's own family of birds and this can be done by selecting pairings consisting of birds with quietness of temperament. This, coupled with the fancier's own even temper and attitude, will do much to ensure good, sound and calm pigeons.

Size is an important matter, especially where the standard dictates a certain size or weight in a breed. Where there is no such standard, there is generally an accepted size and it follows that some birds will be too large and some too small. The pairing of extremes rarely produces average-sized birds, but careful attention to size in the pairs will remove the majority of striking differences. The same applies to feather quality, which, if lacking in a pigeon, can rarely be produced in young pigeons by pairing to a bird with an absolute abundance.

Eye colour is a more complex subject and is determined absolutely by the requirements of particular breed standards. Breeds requiring light eyes will need to be paired accordingly to produce the lightness, whereas breeds in which there is a favour towards depth of colour in the eye will need to be paired with this objective in mind. Experience in breeds will tell the fancier which types of bird will breed those with the eye colouring required. Lightness in eye colour often produces an eye of the very richest hue and much depends upon the family breeding to be able to judge the expectations in eye colouring. Feather colour also dictates most of the ultimate decisions. Self-colours are self-evident, although the mixing of colour often produces depth and richness which cannot be produced by mating like-to-like in colour. In non-standard breeds, of course, there is no colour standard, except that which usually demands that birds can be of any colour providing that it is good, i.e. not faded or lacking in contrast or clarity. Depth of colour is important and, in showing, it is generally accepted that colour must be good. This also holds good for the presence of white feathers in birds, either in flights or in pied markings. In some breeds this is a bar to success, whereas in many it is either disliked entirely or held in high regard by some judges for the non-standard breeds. White will have to be constantly watched, otherwise it can almost become a primary colour, edging out the more acceptable shades and leading to birds becoming extremely gay pieds.

Head shape and expression is another most important consideration. Whatever the breed, a cock should look like a cock and a hen should be sweet enough in expression to tell anyone that it is a female. Expression is most important and to underestimate it is a bad mistake for I feel that many judges place great emphasis upon it. Therefore, breeding pairs should be compatible in this respect so that there is every likelihood of them producing birds which can be sexed by their outward appearance.

Lastly, it is worth stressing that only the most vigorous birds should be bred from, in order to produce birds which are likely to be of good strength. A bird with a sound and robust constitution is far more likely to produce birds of soundness than one which is lacking in substance, listless and not bursting with energy. It is tempting to keep such birds when they conform closely to the standard but really they should be culled so as to remove an apparent weakness.

The only way that such a chapter as this can be rounded up is to end on the same note as was expressed at the beginning, that the decisions regarding pairings are some of the most important to be made within the show loft and the show team. These decisions should therefore be based upon maximum thought and care. These are not overnight decisions, but ones which can take the whole year to formulate.

Chapter 10

Breeding for the Show Team

The breeding programme for show pigeons is very much the same as that for teams of racing pigeons in that the basic care must be applied to produce healthy young pigeons. The vast majority of pigeon literature pertains to the racing pigeon as, throughout the world, it is by far the most numerous of the pigeon breeds and therefore there is much information available.

However, the show loft has minor variations and requirements and it is these that I shall stress during this chapter. Racing-team breeding has to commence in such time as to facilitate the best racing performances out of the racers, with some fanciers preferring to race birds sitting on eggs or feeding youngsters. Therefore timings have to be so arranged. Showing considerations, however, are more simple, although breeding may sometimes have to be fitted in between the main show season in January and the Summer showing season, if one wants to show during both periods.

However, if early showing is not envisaged, then the ending of the breeding season is used to bring on or delay the moult. Breeding will therefore commence as early as mid-December and may go on well into the Summer, possibly as late as August. Showing will greatly affect the choice of time so, therefore, the first decisions are those regarding the best time to commence in order to suit the management of the show loft. In my own case, I usually find that the shows extend well into January and therefore I commence breeding towards the end of that month, allowing as much time as possible to reduce the birds from show fitness down to a body weight more likely to produce top breeding condition. My breeding season will usually end at about the time two rounds of young birds have been produced, although this may be made much later because of the switching of pairings. The normal operation, however, will end in late May although often, when Summer showing is planned, birds will be allowed to sit out pot eggs; this not only ensures fitness but also that their moult is delayed.

In this way, the moult can be delayed considerably to facilitate early shows, even throughout July and into August. When, however, the birds are separated, one must expect a fast and fairly dramatic shedding of feathers, although this never seems to be detrimental, owing to the fitness of the birds following their long rest when sitting on the pot eggs.

The time to commence breeding will, therefore, depend upon such considerations in line with the needs of the loft in question. Let us assume, however, that the need is to breed as soon as possible after the end of the showing season. It is pointless mating the birds when they are in show condition, for generally this means that they are far too fat for comfortable egg-laying. The need, therefore, is to allow sufficient time for the basics to be done to produce the condition so necessary for breeding performance. This does not mean a drastic reduction in food but a gradual reduction in both quantity and in content, with the reduction of the heavy grains such as peas, tares and beans and the inclusion of cereals, especially of barley.

A weekly dose of salts may also be given as a purgative, although this must be done sensibly so as to cause no discomfort. This will also be the time to de-worm the birds and to provide an anti-canker preparation in the drinking water. These are the basic preparations of the birds, which go hand in hand with loft arrangements, such as the installation of nest boxes and the preparation of all other equipment necessary for breeding.

It will be a matter of judgment to decide whether a suitable period has been allowed for the production of breeding condition. Unless it is achieved, however, the first round is likely to be littered with clear eggs and as a result will be a waste of time. Show birds generally are poor breeders compared to racing pigeons, which seem to have far more all-round vigour. Therefore, it is more important than ever to ensure that their condition is right before the breeding operation commences.

It is also important to ensure that the environment is as settled as possible. The more settled the birds are, the better the chances that they will settle together in pairs and get down to the business of breeding and not fight for territory. Steps should therefore be taken to quiet the birds and to assume a form of management which allows this to happen within the loft.

Breeding very early in the year is not natural in that wild birds will wait for the longer days and warmer weather before pairing up and breeding. Pigeon fanciers expect their birds to pair together in the Winter months and give little thought to the fact that it is not a natural time of the year for breeding. To compensate for this somewhat, use can be made of artificial lighting to lengthen the hours of daylight and this will help greatly. Time switches with automatic dimming facilities are available and can be used to give regularity to the lighting. In extreme cold climates, heat may also have to be applied and it follows that much of the ventilation will have to be blanked off. Another useful method in this respect is to provide privacy and warmth by installing a box of some sort within the nest box. This can best be done by either using a hardboard screen of about nest size in one corner of the nest box, or by installing a small cardboard box, just about large enough for the birds to build a nest and to sit their youngsters. As stated, the warmth is assured and often the birds enjoy the privacy.

The key to early breeding, however, is the condition of the pairs, and the aim should be maximum virility and strength without excess fat. This will go most of the way to the production of early eggs and youngsters, although the use of artificial light is also most important to compensate for the shortness of the winter days. If available, heat ensures early production but few fanciers can afford such a luxury, especially in lofts which are built mainly with ventilation in mind.

Nesting material is something which should be given thought. The best and most successful nests are those built by pigeons which can have their liberty and which, as a result, can forage for their material and build their nests, just as birds do in the wild. Nesting pairs will be sublimely happy if allowed their freedom to do this and the resultant condition for breeding is self-evident. However, it is obvious that this is out of the question for the majority of the fancy breeds, especially during the winter season. Birds with flights, however, can be allowed access to the area and given the opportunity to cart material found there to their nests. This is almost taking them back to nature and gives the more active the chance to work at their breeding.

If birds are unable to get outside they tend not to produce very much of a nest at all and will lay in a bare nest bowl. Fanciers will have to be watchful for this and it is a good idea to have a layer of sawdust, wood chippings or sand in each bowl. Twigs and natural foliage are the best materials especially of fir or spruce trees, as they are similar to those which birds would find in their natural environment. Tobacco stalks also are ideal and this material can be purchased at many trade outlets. Generally, birds like the coarser materials in preference to hay and straw. Both these materials should be watched with care as they can harbour disease and insect life. The answer is to place the material in such a place and manner that the birds will want to take it to their nesting places. This will allow them some sort of natural activity which is important to successful breeding. Only where birds fail to build their nests should fanciers install material as a nest for the birds.

The placing of the nest bowls within a box is also worthy of mention. Where nest boxes are arranged symmetrically, it is a good idea to stagger the bowls so that every box has its bowl in a different position. Birds entering a wrong box should immediately realise when they find the bowl somewhere unexpected.

The actual pairing process is very important, for much of the success or otherwise of a breeding operation will depend upon its smoothness. It is of course a matter which is much easier for the fancier with a small team, for not only will his work in the selection of the breeding pairs be more easily accomplished, but getting the birds to pair together will be easier because he can allow more time for each bird. It is most important that fanciers commence pairing their birds when they have as much time as possible available to them.

Showmen often have a distinct advantage in the pairing work because they can use their show pens or cages for the introductions (Figure 34). Birds can be placed in adjacent pens, allowing sight and contact, but in such a manner that no damage is likely to be caused to the hen. This is a most useful manner of pairing birds and is recommended. It is almost an extension of pen training, for the birds should be perfectly at home in the pens and therefore be relaxed.

I have stated elsewhere (p.29) that the larger the nest boxes, the better the chances of successful breeding. This particularly applies to the breeds which are to be entirely confined to their boxes throughout the breeding season, and it goes without saying that such boxes should be large enough, not only in floor area, but also in height, for the birds to be able to properly mate. Where birds, once paired, are to be allowed

Figure 34. Birds being paired in show pens.

in and out of their boxes, it is important to get them settled as soon as possible. The fewer nest boxes in each compartment of the loft the better, especially where these are symmetrically placed in rows. My own use of portable boxes has much to commend it as such boxes can be placed within the loft in such a manner that birds cannot make mistakes of entry. The birds should be introduced to their boxes as quietly as possible, usually with the cocks given their territory first. The hens can then be placed in with their cocks, with one pair being given an open nest-box door, allowing them the freedom into the main compartment, and, where they are flying birds, to the outside world. They will soon realise which is their box and learn to enter that box and no other. Time is so important and, if the changes can be made every hour or so throughout the day, the birds will soon pair quickly and confidently. Often there will be a rogue bird which will insist on entering other boxes and fighting. Such pigeons will have to be given extra time but it is most important that they are dissuaded quickly but without cruelty or loss of temper by the exasperated fancier.

When, and only when, the birds are properly settled to their boxes should the nest bowls be installed. Some fanciers, however, place the bowls in the boxes at the outset, though upside-down so as to allow the hens to shelter from the over-amorous attentions of the cock. The bowls can simply be turned the right way up when the birds are paired.

Where the birds are breeding-fit, eggs should appear on the seventh or eighth day. It is only the clever and experienced fanciers, however, who manage to get all the birds paired and sitting within a ten- to twelve-day period. Fancy pigeons will be especially difficult in this respect, and special thought should be given to the use of feeders (foster parents) and their anticipated laying time in comparison. Normally feeders of the flying breeds will reproduce much more quickly and will therefore need to be paired some days behind the parent birds. It is a good idea to have the feeders in a compartment to themselves to avoid fighting and, of course, cross-fertilisation.

Eggs which are to be switched should be removed as soon after they are laid as possible and safely stored and labelled. They should be replaced with pot eggs and the parents allowed to sit for at least eight days before the pots are removed. Eggs so taken can be stored for seven to ten days in complete safety, provided that they are regularly turned. It is a good idea to place a cross on each (Figure 35) and to ensure that the cross is facing upward one day, out of sight the day following, and so on. The shorter the period of storage the better.

Eggs which are being incubated should be checked for fertility after approximately five days. To the experienced fancier, the mere visual examination will be sufficient as he will note the change of colour from

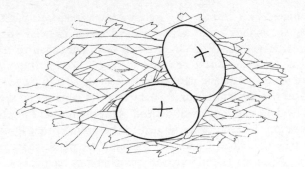

Figure 35. Eggs marked for turning.

near-white to a duller darker hue. Where there is any doubt, however, the eggs should be held up to a light, such as a torch light to establish, as a sign of life, whether the embryo has been formed. This is a good time to examine eggs for cracks or dents – these can be repaired by using adhesive tape, providing that the inner lining of the egg is not ruptured, and by ensuring that the eggs are clean. A minimum amount of fuss should be employed so as to cause as little upset to the sitting birds as possible. When removing eggs for such examination, or later the youngsters for ringing, care should be taken to shield them with the hand so that a defensive wing will cause no damage.

Eggs can be switched from one sitting pair to another providing that hatching dates are within two days of each other. Young pigeons can also be switched with the proviso that the younger they are, the closer their ages should be, although, later in life – from ten days upwards – they can be switched quite successfully and racing men regularly do this to provide maximum race condition and endeavour. I cannot stress too much the importance of keeping very strict records of laying and hatching dates where any switching of eggs and youngsters is to be done. Neither should it be necessary to state the importance of interfering with the nest as little as possible. Many fanciers refuse even to clean the nest box while it is in use, but I tend to clean and freshen every one at least once during each rearing.

I would now like to say a word about culling. When thinking about racing pigeons, considerations about culling are mainly those of strength and vigour. With show birds, however, there are so many more – markings, colour and pigmentation to mention but a few. With ever-rising corn costs, one should always have in mind reducing numbers and the earlier in a bird's life that this is done, the greater the savings. The more experience one develops the better one gets at disposing of the unwanted unlikely show candidates at an early stage. It is rare for the early doubts to be proved wrong later in life. Where

91

young pigeons get chilled, they rarely grow satisfactorily, and where one hatches a long while after its nest mate, likewise they rarely develop satisfactorily. It is far better to seem hard than to rear many birds which will turn out to be wasters.

There is always debate about whether birds should be fed in their nest boxes as a matter of course. Many fanciers believe that this should always be done and much will depend upon the breed of pigeon under consideration. I have always tended to the opinion that birds should always take their food from a central source because there is always waste when corn is placed into nest-box pots (but see p.31 in regard to recessed nest boxes). This is the disadvantage but the obvious advantage is that the young birds will see their parents feeding and will soon copy. I always believe that, as soon as a bird is able to pick up its own food, it should be weaned. It follows, therefore, that my views about the rearing of show birds are to give the parents as little to do as possible, bearing in mind the need for show condition later in the year. Although I tend to prefer hand-feeding at most times of the year, I recommend 'hopper' or 'cafeteria' feeding during the rearing season. Birds should have corn before them at all times when feeding young although I do not believe in feeding them in their nest boxes – unless, of course, the birds are confined to their boxes.

Baths are important for show pigeons at all times of the year and this applies especially during the breeding season, particularly for birds with no access to the outside world. Bathing tones them up and supplies the moisture so necessary to the correct incubation of eggs.

Grit should be in front of the birds at all times, either in special pots or else sprinkled in daily with the food rations. Minerals or salt blocks should also be available and, wherever possible, green food should be offered. Food supplements containing cod liver oil and calcium should be fed when young pigeons are being reared so as to increase the growth rate and produce added vigour. There are proprietory supplements on the market but fanciers can prepare their own, using pin-head oatmeal as a base.

Just as racing enthusiasts think about maximum race performance by their birds, so the showman will have to think about the numbers he wishes to rear from the various pairs. Whilst breeding is a natural function, birds which are over-used in the production of young will soon show the strain and are therefore less likely to regain and maintain maximum condition for the show season. It is a useful aid to have some feeders (see p.13) available to share the burden and often, racing pigeons will make excellent rearers. Also, it is far better to breed from a smaller number of pairs arranged to the expectation of maximum quality, and to use the remainder of the show team as feeders.

Obviously, however, many breeds of fancy show pigeons will need feeders in any case.

The ringing of young pigeons must be performed at just the right time and again experience shows when this should be done. Much depends upon the breed of pigeon and the size of ring to be employed, although the rule seems to be to select an age at which the ring can be applied without discomfort to the bird and yet remain in place. The ring should be applied in such a way that it reads the wrong way up when the bird is standing, but when the bird is in the hand, will read properly and can easily be seen. The youngsters should be placed on a flat surface or even a clean nest bowl and not held in the hand because of considerations of cleanliness. The three front toes should be held together using the thumb and fingers of one hand, while the ring is slipped over these toes using the other hand, with the base of the ring going on first (Figure 36). The ring should be slid along the foot and leg until the back toe is released, thus trapping the ring permanently. No force should be used nor distress caused to the youngsters. In the event of the ring being a tighter fit than usual, a lubricant should be used such as petroleum jelly.

When the young birds are old enough, they should be weaned well away from their parents or any other old birds which may have assumed the feeding role. They can be placed on the floor of a spare compartment, with access to water, and given food of their normal

Figure 36. Ringing a young bird.

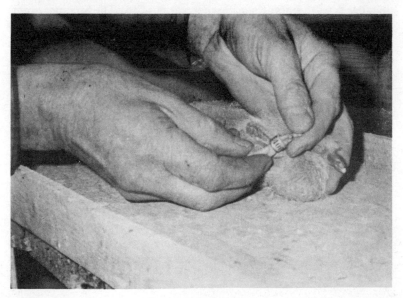

93

mixture. They may seem to go hungry for a while but nature will take over and they will feed hungrily when they feel the need. Young show pigeons can also be weaned to the show pens and this then serves a double advantage in allowing them early and lasting use of the pens. It is worthwhile to wean birds in groups wherever possible, thus giving them the opportunity to learn from each other.

The breeding season is the most interesting time within the loft for success or otherwise later in the year at the shows will be determined upon the successful breeding of quality youngsters. The principles are varied but one should avoid over-breeding from the show candidates so as to allow them every chance of sustaining show condition. It is also a mistake to breed too many youngsters to cause overcrowding.

It is a good idea to work out a plan at the start of the breeding operation, stating how many youngsters are wanted from each pairing and to accommodate plans accordingly. Thought will also have to be given to the splitting of some pairings so that the birds can be re-paired as a means of testing the potential of birds as breeders, and to using birds of proven breeding ability to best advantage. Such plans may not always be fulfilled but are important in deciding one's needs at the outset.

As stated earlier (p.86), one of the considerations in the timing of the commencement and conclusion of the breeding season will be the showing programme. In the absence of shows, one will be able to enjoy the luxury of pairing the birds when it suits most, according to weather conditions or convenience. Where shows are anticipated, it is necessary to tailor dates to suit the shows wherever possible. The Summer events are enjoyable ones and the breeding programme can be usefully employed to retard the moult. In any case, when the required numbers are reared, it is good for the birds to be able to sit out a pair of pot eggs, so that they can be rested in readiness for the moult and showing season.

Breeding is the key to good fanciership and to good showing. Thought, planning and hard work must be applied at all times and then hopefully, success will follow.

Chapter 11

Judges and Judging:
Some Observations

Very few people will admit that they are bad drivers and, likewise few pigeon fanciers will admit that they are poor at judging pigeons. Yet, in the main, for what is the most important part of pigeon showing, scant regard is paid to the many considerations which apply to the appointment of judges to shows. There is little point in paying great attention to show organisation, seeing to minute detail, then to fail the fancier in not providing judges of sufficient calibre. Bad judging will ruin a show both for organisers and exhibitors alike.

It is now many years since I first judged a pigeon show and I can honestly say that I have learned something from every judging appointment since. Every occasion has presented a challenge of the sort that demands thought and attention to detail, together with a fair amount of preparation.

Over the years, I have also taken the opportunity of studying hundreds of judges at work on their respective breeds and can only conclude that judging standards throughout the world are wildly short of the professionalism which the showing of pigeons deserves. This applies more especially to the non-standard breeds, where results, as often as not, take on the form of a lottery.

At a guess, I would say that most fanciers who read this chapter will already have done some judging and can therefore reflect on whether or not what I am saying is true. The newcomer who has yet to face the trauma of selecting birds for the prize cards, can perhaps bear it all in mind for future reference and reflection.

A first judging appointment is always a little nerve-tingling, as well as an honour, and it is always, to some extent, a measure of the esteem in which one is held by fellow fanciers. Often the newcomer is slow and hesitant and can easily panic when faced with the reality of judging a large number of birds within a relatively short time. Later on in one's judging career, confidence builds and then the biggest danger of all is present – nonchalance. The judge who feels that he knows it all and can easily deal and dispense with all that appears before him, is the worst of his kind for he is liable to sacrifice detail in a desire to appear knowledgeable and speedy, thus giving a poor return to both exhibitor and show organisers – and also the poor pigeons. The good judge,

Figure 37. Black Dragoon.

however, will appear unhurried, with one steady pace, dealing with everything in turn and in a set manner. He gives every entry a chance by applying time to it. He will be the person in constant demand at future shows.

Without a doubt there are as many poor judges as good ones and I feel very strongly that the quality of judging is a subject that should be discussed freely and openly. After all, there is no point in grumbling behind a judge's back and suffering in wounded silence.

The judge's decisions are always final – that is the first elementary rule we all learn, but they are not beyond criticism; they never have been and hopefully never will become so.

What therefore makes a good judge? It is certainly not a case of the best and most successful of exhibitors and breeders being good at judging, for some of these fanciers make the worst of judges. Indeed, some of the best judges are those who have retired from the sport, or passed on to other breeds, yet maintain what is best described as a sympathy or feeling for the breed. This brings me to the related subject of whether judges should be current fanciers of the breed in question. Arguments have raged over this for many years and will, of course, never be resolved. My own feeling is that it is desirable but not essential, providing that the sympathy or understanding is maintained – and by maintained I also mean kept-up-to-date.

Figure 38. German Helmet.

How, therefore, do we overcome this mystique, this illusion of the unassailable knowledge and power of judges? In Britain, the situation is made much worse by the secrecy which surrounds a judge and his actions, for in only a few shows can the exhibitor actually witness the judging procedures. Contrast this with the USA, where the emphasis is on openness and the spectator value of the judging. Having experienced both methods, I can say with certainty that the latter has much more to commend it because it immediately removes the mystery and allows the exhibitor to see how his birds are being dealt with. Those interested can observe the judge and determine, by his actions, whether he can be considered capable. Indecisions will be noted, as will slowness, panic or other obvious failings. In Britain, in most cases, the only person who would be able to spot such matters would be the steward or helper, a person connected with the show but normally unconnected with the breed being judged at that time.

Observation of the judging by the showmen can be no finer check against incompetence, and also combats any chance of cheating, although this happens on only very few occasions. Let things be done

Figure 39. Norwich Cropper.

openly, let them be seen to be done, and then standards can be raised accordingly. I am all for overt judging, for allowing the operation to be seen so that the best and most competent judges can be recognised as such and therefore used to the best advantage in furthering the sport of pigeon showing and raising standards overall.

Let me say at this point that, while I like to see good judges doing their work regularly, there should be a good selection of judges available, not only to give experience to newcomers, but also to ensure that breeds can be allowed to modify or change slowly, in accordance with popular demand. If judging is in the hands of too few individuals, they are likely to prevent this happening and, indeed, hold a breed back through their inability to modernise and adapt. I appreciate that, for standard breeds, the contrary argument can be used but I sincerely believe that, whatever standard is set, it will tend to be modified and improved over the years, and that this should be allowed to happen. Nevertheless, it should be a slow process and in accordance with the will of the majority.

In this context, I feel that successful exhibitors should judge

Figure 40. Exhibition Flying Tippler.

whenever asked. This is a sacrifice, especially if one is keen on the exhibition side and motivated by the desire to win, but there is the wider responsibility owed to the sport to lend the expertise and knowledge of one's own breed. This is undoubtedly the best way of keeping showing professional and removing much of the lottery aspect which exists especially in the non-standard breeds.

The other advantage, however, is that the judge will gain a great deal by each and every judging experience and will thus be able to increase his own knowledge of his breed. It is a form of checking his own progress within the sport and, perhaps more importantly, as an opportunity to compare the efforts of his future rivals.

In talking about judges and judging methods in pigeon showing, it is difficult to be too general because showing is divided into two main categories: a) standard breeds and b) non-standard varieties, which includes the showing of racing pigeons, which is a different matter again. For each, a different method of judging must be applied.

Standard Breeds

These are the popular breeds of fancy pigeon for which there is prescribed a breed standard, written and probably illustrated. In most cases also, there will be a club, secretary or organisation catering for the breed, representing it and furthering its progress.

Where the standard is prescribed in detail, there is also a good chance that judging methods and markings are likewise prescribed, with each point of the standard taking a set number of marks. It is therefore a matter of the judge going through the standard and marking the bird accordingly, adding the totals at the conclusion and awarding the cards bearing the result. Often the standard system of marking gives instruction on deducting marks for such matters such as lack of condition, the presence of dirt or insect life and other faults more attributable to the exhibitor than the bird being judged.

When judging to a standard, it goes without saying that any judge must always have the set standard very much in mind. (Regretfully, I have even seen judges at mixed breed shows referring to illustrated books to ensure that breeds not entirely familiar to them are given a fair judgement.) Providing that the standard is constantly borne in mind, there is little way in which a judge can go wrong, although it must be said that, in the end, it all comes down to the judge's opinion on how closely the bird being appraised conforms to the written statement.

The most likely cause for dispute will be when condition on the day is involved. This may happen, for instance, when a bird closely resembling the official standard, but out-of-sorts or not in absolute show condition, is compared unfavourably with a bird in tip-top condition but with faults within the confines of the standard. If these faults are minor ones, then the problem becomes more acute.

Figure 41. West of England Flying Tumbler.

Figure 42. Pigmy Pouter.

Judging at specialist breed shows is very important to the breed and its progress. Judges will normally be selected for their knowledge of the breed and there is little room for manoeuvre. The standard is all important and must be applied. It is not up to a judge to apply his own interpretation of the standard; that is already a matter for records, although judges will shape a breed by a very gradual preference which might ultimately lead to the governing body making amendments to breed standards.

Non-standard Breeds

This term refers to all other breeds of pigeons not catered for by a written standard and includes show racers, racing pigeons, flying breeds of fancy pigeon and all other breeds, some popular and others rare.

Judging of classes of non-standard breeds is a far different matter, and the judge's opinion on the day is the only one which counts. Here, type and condition will be the two main considerations, with colour perhaps coming next in line. Every judge will have his own ideas as to the type he is looking for within the breed under consideration. He will have no specific written standard to adhere to but will be aware of the finer points and what is generally expected by way of convention and precedent.

In many breeds, such as show racers and flying fancy breeds,

Figure 43. Damascene Ice Blue cock.

handling properties will have great importance, with type forming a very significant part. (Type refers not only to the outward appearance of the bird, but also to its handling properties and involves balance, body and feather.)

Type is extremely important and is far more likely to be recognised if the bird is in the peak of show condition. Therefore, the condition of the bird on the day takes on equal importance and, I would assert, has far more bearing on the judging of non-standard breeds than of standard varieties. The very best of pigeons, if not in the peak of condition, will appear merely ordinary, whereas the reverse applies and absolute condition can cover or hide faults in basic make-up.

Fanciers who keep standard breeds argue that the judging of the non-standards is more of a lottery and perhaps, to some extent, this is true. This is why the greatest care should be taken in the selection of judges, who should be fanciers with the ability to find the best birds on the day. Those who deride written standards argue that the flexibility granted by the absence of the written rule is the best avenue to ensure development in line with accepted desire.

The judging of the non-standards, however, is a more difficult matter and a far greater overall knowledge is required, as there is no written standard available for reference. The essentials of a good judge,

Figure 44. A show racer champion owned by the author.

therefore, are overall knowledge coupled with an up-to-date awareness of developments and movements within a breed. Certainly a judge is less open to criticism for it is very much a case of his preference on the day, his likes and dislikes and, in the end, his own decision. I have indicated earlier that the judging of racing pigeons – birds which have either genuinely raced distances or are being judged on their ability to do so, presents a slightly different problem. The same may be said of flying breeds in classes where flying ability counts more than show properties. Let us confine ourselves to the racers, however, for these are by far the most numerous in terms of shows and showing. The point I wish to make is that birds entered in genuine racing, diploma or performance classes cannot be always judged to show standards of requirements. Judges will have to make allowances for the scars of performance, the frets and other matters, which show even long after

Figure 45. English Short-faced Tumbler.

Figure 46. Nun

the performance. The wise judge will remember this while making his selections and make allowances commensurate with the strains involved. Likewise, if the class is for racing pigeons likely to win and race – say over 500 miles – he will most certainly have to consider whether the physical construction of the birds before him is adequate to equip them for such an undertaking. It will be pointless applying many of the showing considerations – except perhaps fitness – to the birds in the class, because showing marks will not carry the bird many of those 500 miles.

These are some of the considerations facing judges and, quite clearly, there is a great deal of difference in judging those breeds with the standards and those without. However, whatever the breed of pigeon to be judged, I say with certainty that all show fanciers ought to be looking for ways to improve the professionalism of judges and their judging methods. There is no point in staging shows without taking the extra care to provide the good, knowledgeable and competent judges.

Judging will not be improved by secrecy or an unwillingness to discuss the practical issues involved. I would like to see far more debate and openness so that the views of the majority can be sought. This especially applies to breed clubs who might well benefit by organising 'teach-ins', to build up an expertise in those acceptable as judges of the breed in question.

In the non-standard breeds, this presents slightly more difficulties but the problems are not insurmountable. The biggest problems arise in the showing of racing pigeons because of the diverse views of the thousands of fanciers within that section of the sport. It is most difficult to merge the aims and ideals of those who prefer to show with those who see the racer merely and solely as a racing machine. Education is the only hope here, to break down the barriers of prejudice and ignorance which often exists.

I hope that this chapter will have been useful as a means of airing some of the views and ideals which are regularly portrayed and debated. The aim always, however, in the interests of the showing of pigeons, should be to increase the competence of the judges so that the quality of the birds being shown can be ever-improving.

Chapter 12

Judging Pigeons:
Practical Considerations

In the preceding chapter, I deliberately discussed the subject of judging in general terms without coming to the object of the exercise — how to do it, or how it might be performed.

It is impossible to cover in detail all the intricacies of judging each and every breed of pigeon shown throughout the world, and also the variations in the methods of showing and judging of those breeds in each and every country, but certain matters are standard. Perhaps the most obvious is that of the appearance, as well as the competence, of the judge. I have constantly made reference to the raising of standards within this sport of ours and one way in which this can be achieved is to have judges who not only perform the task well, but look a credit to the sport when they are doing it. There is little worse than to see a slopy, untidy individual wandering up and down the show pens, looking dishevelled or unkempt and perhaps with a cigarette hanging out of his mouth.

It is a fairly simple matter for judges to present themselves looking clean and tidy, wearing a suitable judging coat over their normal clothing and with a suitable stick or other implement with which the birds to be judged can be made to position themselves.

There can be no fixed way of judging but within every breed there will be the usual accepted way which any judge will have picked up over the years by watching others. This is the usual way of learning the craft — by the careful study of those with more experience and the selection from them of aspects which seem suitable and in accordance with one's own style.

I always feel that it is a good idea at the commencement of any class, whether standard or non-standard, to take an initial look through the birds in the class, as a means of fixing the numbers involved and to gauge the overall quality, reflecting the likely task involved in ultimately sorting them out.

This initial check is an important one because first impressions are generally the right ones and give a good pointer to the more detailed examination to follow. It is a good idea at this stage to use the stick to get the birds to stand correctly and it is surprising just how many of the older and more experinced birds tend to relax onto one wing, even in

Figure 47. Indian Fantail Self White cock.

the early stages of a show. This initial check, of course, applies mainly to birds which are to be judged in their pens and has less significance if the birds are to be taken to the judge at a table, or if a 'walking pen' is used.

Following the initial examination, there then follows the main task, when the birds are examined, in turn, in greater detail. Some breeds, and some classes within breeds, are not handled when being judged and, therefore, the task for the judge is in defining those birds nearest to the standard, where there is one, or to his liking in the non-standard breed classes. Here too, condition will play an important part and any good judge should be able to appreciate and recognise the very peak of show condition in the birds under him. In such classes, the use of the stick will be quite important in getting the birds to show themselves to their best – or to reveal their worst points.

More commonly, however, birds are handled. The judge should try to be calm and deliberate in movement with a similar approach to each pigeon and no sudden movement to startle it. It is a bad enough ordeal for pigeons to be placed in show pens in artificial and strange surroundings, especially for the young and inexperienced, but judges who grab at them really add to the problems overall. I have seen judges who have reduced a class of birds to a state of near-wildness because of

Figure 48. Tung Koon Paak Self White cock.

their lack of expertise and consideration. They seem to have had little or no idea how to remove a pigeon from its pen.

There is no set way of doing this, except that it is most important to be able to get the bird out without it damaging itself in any way. When judging, it is always a thrill to find a really tame bird who almost asks to be picked out and one has to do but a small amount of judging to realise just how important pen training is. Some judges prefer to pick the bird from underneath, placing the hand under the bird and holding it firmly with the thumb so that it is unable to flap the wings in the crucial removal. Others prefer to place the hand over the rump, holding wings, tail and legs in the grasp of one or both hands. Once in the hand, each pigeon should be treated with care and respect and held in such a way that escape is impossible – usually with the thumb over the rump and the index and second finger securely holding the legs.

The judging method will be determined by the type of bird. The standard breed will be checked for standard considerations and the judgement will be mainly visual, whereas the flying and racing breeds will be sorted not only visually but also by handling properties. Indeed, where the body and balance plays such an important part of the judgement, it is said that most of the decisions are made by feel at waist level before the bird is held up for visual examination at eye level.

The system used must be one which allows the same sort of time for each pigeon and one which allows the judge to judge and record the matters important to the overall pigeon. Marking systems vary greatly. Some are elaborate and cater for various points of the bird, especially those used in the standard breeds. However, even in the non-standard breeds judges evolve their own marking cards or sheets, sometimes making the process almost as mathematical as practical.

Others use a very simple system of ticks or crosses and I must confess that I favour this simple way. During my initial check of a class, I give a tick to those birds I like and, when I handle the candidates later, each bird liked at that stage is given a further tick or two and, in exceptional cases, even more. This removes the need to compute scores and I am always fearful of changing values, especially in very large classes.

Examples of cards or score sheets which I have seen in use, are given in Figures 49 and 50. The first is an old one from many years ago which was mainly used for racing pigeons. Each bird had a card completed for it by the judge and was given a score. Cards were then

Figure 49. An authentic judging card used in racing pigeon shows.

SECTIONS	POSSIBLE NO. OF POINTS	NO. OF POINTS AWARDED	REMARKS
STANCE Appearance in Pen.	5		
HEAD Shape and Structure, Colour & Condition of Eye.	5		
WINGS Primaries, Secondaries, Cover Feathers etc.	5		
BODY Conformation, Balance, Condition, etc.	5		
TAIL Tail and general Feathering.	5		
EYE-SIGN ◎	10		
Total No. of Possible Points	35		Total No. of Points awarded

CLASS   **PEN No.**

BRITISH STANDARD

THIS CARD IS THE COPYRIGHT OF
ALL BRITISH PIGEON RACING GAZETTE
BANK CHAMBERS, MARKET PLACE
KINGSTON ON THAMES, SURREY, ENGLAND.

ASSESSMENT CARD

Pen No.:

Excellence

Requirements

Faults (severe)

Disqualifications

GRADE.. Condition..

PRIZE/S..

Grade Key: 'E'=Excellent 'O'=Outstanding
'VG'=Very Good 'G'=Good
'U'=Unsatisfactory 'W'=Worthless

Figure 50. A modern assessment card which is attached to each pen after judging.

displayed on the show pen. The second is a more up-to-date form which is used by a well-known judge of fancy and rare varieties. A form is completed for each pigeon and displayed upon the show pen. It does not mark but grades and it takes courage to be so open and direct. It is perhaps the best form of open judging which can be envisaged. In some of the Continental countries the pointing and marking systems are quite elaborate and great emphasis seems to be placed on them.

I have always taken my judging seriously and have appreciated the tiring aspect of it. Large classes are usually the most difficult and anything over fifty entries demands a great deal of effort on the part of the judge. I feel that one hundred and fifty to two hundred birds is the most that any fancier should be asked to judge in a day. I well recall being asked to judge nearly five hundred pigeons in twenty classes at the Young Bird National Show in Louisville, Kentucky (Figure 51), and found this to be a most tiring operation. The task took all day, despite the fact that there was the ever-present need to move without haste. At the end of the day I was absolutely shattered and left to hope that tiredness had not affected the decisions too badly.

Figure 51. The author judging at the Young Bird National Show, Louisville, Kentucky.

Each judge should be given a commitment which allows him sufficient time to judge each bird so that every entry gets a chance. Every bird should be considered, even those which appear to have no earthly chance of success.

I would like to refer to some points which can cause consternation to judges. What does one do with a very wild pigeon which refuses to be handled, or which when placed in a judging pen upsets and frightens others? Such birds, I feel, will undoubtedly be discarded without too much argument, as it is a poor reflection on the fanciership of the exhibitor.

Birds found to be carrying insect life also present a problem. This varies between standard and non-standard breeds and generally means disqualification in the latter but with the standard taking overall precedence in the former. Indeed, I am often shocked and disappointed at the state in which some fancy pigeons are exhibited, pointing to lack of basic care or indifference on the part of their owners.

What does a judge do when he finds marked pigeons entered? By this I mean plastic rings, name and address stamps or other means of

Figure 52. Tunisian Owl Self Black hen.

identification or marking. Probably the best course here is for the judge to request a steward to remove the offending marking, otherwise the judge is open to criticism by other exhibitors.

I am always saddened to find judges who tend to 'fault-judge' by happily discarding birds they can fault in some minute detail, e.g. a fret. This, of course, mainly applies to the non-standard breeds but it is most annoying because often poorer specimens are placed ahead of good birds simply because of the presence of a minor fret, or piece of dirt, etc. I believe that any fault should be considered but that the object of the exercise for any judge is to judge the bird overall and not to try to be clever to discover minor blemishes.

What should the judge do when he finds birds which are slightly dirty, having soiled themselves in some way, either in the show pen or on the way to the show? Here again, I tend always to advise that allowances should be made for such matters, because it is not a fault in construction. It might count against a bird which is equal in every other respect to another bird but in no way should a bird be marked down, allowing poorer specimens to gain prizes, simply because they have escaped without such minor marking blemishes.

Another matter which should be mentioned here is the deliberate fixing of faults, sometimes more extremely called faking. These include feather trimming or transplanting, colouring of feathering, feet, beaks or other parts and, indeed, any other act which changes the appearance of the bird in some way. This is almost the subject of a separate chapter but again a great deal depends on the rules and precedent in each breed. Certainly in show racers and racing pigeons, a great deal of this goes on and, as far as Britain is concerned, there is nothing written against it, although many judges will mark down in some degree birds they find so treated. In other breeds, rules prohibit such practices and, when they are discovered, the judge will have little alternative but to act in accordance with those rules. I have certainly seen some very professional cosmetic improvements to pigeons, including the skilful transplantation of primary, secondary or tail feathers. Some trimming jobs are most difficult to spot and, of course, the larger the number of birds in a class, the less likelihood there is of discovery.

A good experienced judge at work is worth seeing for he will be using all the experience gained through numerous previous engagements. He will seem unhurried, unflustered and in complete command of the situation. Many judges will handle a pigeon only once but this depends on the numbers available in the class under him. Small classes are obviously easier to judge and, where there are over fifty birds, then the judge will need either a super memory or plenty of time and a willing note-taker as a steward. I do not like to see pigeons handled too freqeuently, as it upsets them and reduces their chances by removing show bloom or lustre. Once or twice should be quite sufficient for most cases.

Larger classes can be quite difficult to sort out and often I find that an energy crisis arises at about halfway. It is often a good idea then to take a walk, enjoy a change of scenery or to have a cup of coffee as a means of relaxation.

I have already mentioned judging over five hundred pigeons in a day. The logistics of this are quite frightening when one relates the time available to the number of birds and classes, as well as taking into consideration the award of the special prizes at the end. In that particular case, I judged in both British and American ways in that each class was sorted as follows. In each class the birds were placed in two rows of pens and initially judged in the British style, in their respective pens. However, two large 'walking pens' were provided into which I placed the birds I wished to consider for awards. After this initial judging, I was generally left with seven to ten birds in each of the two larger pens.

These birds in these pens were then judged American-style. As the classification was strictly by colour division, e.g. blue-bar classes, dark-chequer classes and so on, and hopefully by judging to type, I was often left with a number of birds in the pens which looked almost identical

Figure 53. The National Show, White Plains, New York, with judging in progress.

and from these I had to select the prize-winners. With time ever-pressing, I felt that I had more than my share of problems on that day! It was probably the hardest judging appointment I have ever had, or am ever likely to have, but it taught me a great deal and, despite tiredness, I was extremely happy about it all.

Judging should always be enjoyed. Providing that a set course is adopted, allowing for fairness to all concerned, including the exhibitor and the pigeons, then there is no reason why every judging appointment should not be an enjoyable experience. An expertise will thus be built to the benefit of the sport of showing in general. Thought should be given to the task to be performed, however, because pre-planning will assist in the work to be performed in the show hall. Every part of judging should be treated seriously so that the nonchalance previously mentioned can always be avoided.

It has often been said that good judges are few and far between but the aim of all judges should be to raise standards and to allow more people to acquire the professionalism needed to further the showing of pigeons.

Chapter 13

Show Organisation

Pigeon shows come in all shapes and sizes but, whatever the size, from the smallest and most modest event to the largest and most prestigious, the show will be far better if the correct amount of thought and planning has been applied. When talking about show organisation, an old colleague of mine has always had an expression to the effect that if the small matters are looked after and given consideration then the main ones will look after themselves.

I believe this to be largely true in that as much thought as possible should be applied to the minor details which are so important to making any show a complete success and I shall set out some of the considerations involved in show organisation in the hope that they will act as a guide for anyone setting out on the road to show organisation.

In broad outline, shows generally take on the following forms:

(a) Club Shows Small events organised by clubs and societies and open only to local membership.

(b) Small Open or Semi-restricted Shows Events organised by clubs or societies but which are thrown open to fellow societies or members within the prescribed areas.

(c) Inter-club or Society Shows These are shows which are open to the members of Societies involved in the competition but not open to other fanciers.

(d) Open Shows Events open to fanciers anywhere.

(e) Classic Events Shows of considerable standing within the national calendar of pigeon showing.

I shall aim my thoughts towards the organisation of open shows as these are probably the most common and perhaps the most difficult to organise as a whole. In so doing, I expect that what I have to say will be pertinent to organisers of all the other types of show. The larger scope of the open show will tax the talents of any show organiser and, by the same token, is likely to offer the most number of pitfalls.

Generally, the organisation for a show commences from the very moment that members or the committee of a club or society decide that a show is to be held. At this stage, more often than not, decisions are made as to the type of show and its scope, with particular regard being paid to the venue and date, the style and size of the show, its classification and likely costings, including entry fees and prize money or special awards. At this time, due regard should be paid to these points and to the needs and consensus of the membership in general. In other words, does the membership wish to have a prestigious general event, an event confined to themselves, or do they wish it to be kept to a small event not openly attracting outsiders.

The guide lines prescribed at such a meeting will be vague and general in nature and, in most cases, the finer detail will be left to an organising committee of elected members. The election of such a committee is vital to the future success of the show and, as in most other facets of life, a good volunteer is worth more than several pressed men.

When the committee meets, it should start by considering the general criteria imposed for the show and deciding whether arrangements can be made to suit these criteria. The committee must have regard for the size and scope of the show and should also take the overall budget into consideration. Pigeon shows, like all other events in life, are subject to inflation and ever-increasing expenses. It is at this very early stage that a rough or draft budget should be produced, outlining the likely expenses and sources of income and suggesting whether the books can be balanced at the conclusion of the show. If there is likely to be a surplus, whether it be large or small, then there is little need for reference back to the main society but, if there is doubt as to the viability, then there will have to be further discussion.

Any successful committee, having worked out the confines of the show and its likely budget, will then consider the delegation of responsibility. Members will know that they are working within the confines of the decisions made by the show society in general but members of the committee should be deputed to take over the organisation of certain aspects of the show within those terms. I will deal with delegation more fully later (p.124), but I have absolutely no doubt that the success or failure of any show depends very much upon the decisions taken at this time. By removing much of the work from the shoulders of the man in overall charge − generally the secretary − he can supervise the work of others and draw the whole together, prior to, and at, the show.

Having set the scene, consideration can now be given to the more specific aspects of the show organisation, and these can be listed as follows.

Date

Generally, open shows are 1-day events prescribed by overall expense and requirements. However, if open shows develop into large-scale events, then consideration has to be given to making them into 2-day shows. This will allow for the larger numbers to be adequately judged and give exhibitors and spectators a better chance to see the birds. The choice of a date, however, is no easy matter and will be affected not only by the availability and cost of the hall, which may well be more reasonable on some days than others, but also by the proximity either of large classic events or of other shows or fixtures in the locality. It would be pointless to hold a show within days of any prestigious classic event, nor is it sensible to hold a show which clashes with a more established and popular event nearby. Many other factors also come into play when thinking about dates, such as the state of the moult and the availability of judges, suitable pens and staging, as well as helpers to work at the show.

Venue

The availability of the show hall on the date in question is one of the foremost considerations and often presents a 'chicken and egg' situation where the date might drastically affect and decide the choice of hall and *vice versa*. The venue is a most important choice and, for a large open show, the best possible should be obtained within the confines of available funds. Whilst smaller shows and club shows can be arranged in smaller more cramped accommodation, the success or otherwise of a large open show will depend upon the facilities open to those attending. The facilities have to be good and airy with sufficient ventilation and lighting (natural light if possible, and heating or ventilation arrangements suitable for the time of the year) and with good refreshment facilities, not only for members of the public and exhibitors, but for entertaining the judges. Consideration will also have to be given to the position of the hall i.e. whether it is within reach of the majority of exhibitors, can be reached by bus or train services or has good parking arrangements.

The hall should be big enough to allow plenty of space for the pens to be staged – wherever possible in single tier and with plenty of space between to allow for ease of access and viewing. The more space the better for this purpose and the wider the area of the show hall the more flexibility there is to include other attractions, such as trade stands and

Figure 54. General view of the Young Bird National Show, Louisville, Kentucky.

displays in conjunction with the show. Although the general principle in Britain is that spectators are not allowed in while judging is in progress, I feel that this is a great pity and would like to see more provision made for viewing the judging procedures as in the USA and other countries.

A refreshment room should be set aside and the provision of alcoholic refreshment is a means of additional income to the show and a further attraction to those attending. It also helps the secretary considerably if he is able to have a room set aside from the main bustle of the show so that he can get on with his work in comparative peace. All these considerations will affect the choice of venue and my advice would be to have the best available for the cash available. A good venue will enhance future prospects whereas the opposite can almost condemn a show from the start.

Classification

Arguments always abound regarding the number and type of classes to be offered. Classification will vary between the small club shows, which may be one- or two-class events, right through to the large shows trying to cater for various breeds. Where numerous breeds are involved, the number of classes will quickly amount to hundreds but, again confining my thoughts to open shows, the aim at this time should be to strike a good balance.

Where shows cater for one or two breeds, then the matter is relatively easy as, generally, classification is fairly well defined to allow for the various divisions or colour considerations within the breed.

Thought, however, will have to be applied to the provision of an attractive classification to bring entries into the show, one which is wide enough to do this and yet allows the organising committee sufficient scope to keep the classification within the bounds of existing or available funds. It is a diverse and interesting exercise and one which will be further complicated by the need to separate the sexes and, further, to separate old birds from young birds.

Generally-speaking, I would say that, in Britain, the aim appears to be to keep the numbers of classes down and the numbers of entries up, whereas, in many other countries, where the classification is divided first into colour, e.g. blue bar, dark chequer, and then into four, to cater for cocks, hens, young birds and old birds, it will be readily seen that the numbers can soon build up. I, therefore, feel that the more numerous the classifications, the less valuable the competition and ultimate prestige.

Judges

This is another subject which provokes argument, sentiment and occasionally outright prejudice. Much thought will have to be given to the provision of judges because good judges will attract a wide and varied entry, thus adding to the prestige of the show and its likely success as a venue for competition. Judges should be selected for their ability to do the job professionally and competently and in good time.

They should also be selected for their overall fairness so that equal opportunity is given to fanciers living in the locality of the show and to those who are likely to travel for the event. Consideration will also have to be given to the likely cost for, if expenses are to be offered, and this is often necessary to attract suitable judges, then the cumulative sum may cause embarrassment to the organising committee. The larger the show, the bigger the problem is likely to be in this respect. However, as a matter of courtesy, the suitable and adequate entertainment of chosen judges should always be allowed for.

Prize Money

If prize money is to be offered, then the amounts have to be budgeted for at an early stage, in line with the numbers of classes available.

Shows not offering prize money will have to cater for the attractions on offer by way of prize cards, rosettes, ribbons or other prizes.

Gauging whether the likely outcome in prize money or specials can be recouped by the show in general, including the level of entry fees, is a matter of pure economics. Entry fees for each exhibit will have to be sufficiently high to finance the show but low enough not to deter would-be exhibitors. Again, there is a delicate balance.

Admission Charges

The largest shows could not operate without admission charges at the door. However, for most other shows, a definite decision has to be made at an early stage as to whether admission is to be charged. Economics come into play in this decision for, if a charge is to be made, then the door has to be manned throughout the duration of the show and this can be expensive in man-hours. Many shows will dispense with an admission charge but hope to raise money by organising draws or raffles. Most people attending such events fully appreciate the need for such fund-raising to finance the overall organisation.

Stationery

This includes all the various paraphernalia necessary to allow the show to run smoothly. It is an expensive part of any show and includes prize cards, judging books, pen labels, basket labels and so on. There are sources of such stationery to be found but, of course, expense is a key factor. For instance, prize cards can be purchased in general form and the name of the show can be added either by hand or by a rubber stamp. Alternatively, they can be printed for the particular show. For many exhibitors a well-presented prize card is a great attraction and one which will doubtless encourage entrants who might not otherwise bother to exhibit.

Advertisements

Thought will have to be given on how to publicise the show. Advertisements can be placed in the various pigeon magazines at reasonably economic rates and these can take the form either of a short specific advertisement or of a full-scale representation of the classification, so that exhibitors can enter from the full advertisement. The latter has the advantage of dispensing with the need for a printed schedule but can itself be expensive, depending upon the scale of the classification. Advertisement can also be effected by letters or circulars to all clubs in the area and even by local newspapers, radio or television.

Schedule

The schedule takes various forms and as mentioned above can be included in pigeon-magazine advertisements. The more common method, however, is for show organisers to have their schedule printed by professionals or run off on a duplicating machine. Another alternative is to photocopy a page or two-page style schedule. The scale of the show largely dictates the type of schedule to be employed, although again printing costs will do much to determine this.

Stewards

Any show will need a set number of stewards or helpers to see it through. An organisation putting on a show will know, at a fairly early stage, its likely pool of helpers. Sad to say, this work always seems to be done by the same few, while their efforts are enjoyed by the majority. It is always a good idea to show some appreciation of those who do the work by offering them free refreshment or other simple reward within the show.

Penning

The availability of suitable penning arrangements is a great consideration. Many clubs and organisations own their own pens but others have to rely on hiring them from firms or from other organisations or clubs. Indeed, large shows may have to rely on hiring pens from various organisations in the locality.

This can be expensive and time-consuming, as well as throwing additional responsibility on the organisers. Transport of the pens to and from shows also has to be considered and budgeted for, in terms not only of cash but also man-hours. Suitable staging also has to be procured and much of the success or otherwise of a show depends on adequate and suitable staging arrangements. Much thought should be given to attractive planning of penning arrangements; suitable paper should be used under the pens to protect the staging, between the pens to prevent pigeons being able to peck at each other and to separate the cocks from the hens and also to add to the overall attraction of the show.

Feed and Water

Shows held in fairly confined areas, and within fairly confined hours, may not have to provide food and water for the birds. However, in a show which is a full-day event, and which attracts fanciers from long distances, there should be provision for watering and feeding the birds.

It goes without saying that any show taking longer than a day obviously needs good feeding and watering arrangements. I have very set ideas on such arrangements. I maintain that any show taking a full day, with penning possibly being done on the previous evening, demands that every pigeon should be fed and watered and I prefer this to be done prior to judging. In my view, it is a good idea for each pen to have a small drinker partially filled with water and a very small quantity of corn or seed available in each pen. This gives every fancier the same chance, not only those travelling very long distances but also those coming from the immediate locality. Access to food and water relaxes the birds and allows their digestive functions to operate in a natural manner, thus reducing the stress imposed on them.

Security

I regard this as one of the main considerations of the organisers of any important open show. Thought should be given to adequate security of baskets, crates or other receptacles, for the securing of pens following judging, the provision of night-watchmen and stewards at the show who should be on the alert for any likely theft. Nothing detracts from a show more than to see lax security and much thought should be given to this particular item. It is always a good rule to state categorically that no bird will be handled at the show other than in the presence of an official steward. If this rule were to be applied at all large shows, much of the opportunity to steal birds would be removed.

Post-show Period

I have briefly mentioned the necessity for an adequate number of stewards and helpers and this particularly applies at the clearing-up stage. Many hands make light work and it is worth the trouble of any show organiser to ensure that he has suitable helpers at the conclusion of the show to ensure that all is cleared up quickly and properly.

As soon after the show as possible, the committee should meet to discuss and digest the show and be in a position to criticise what has occurred, with a view to making adjustments and improvements in future events. The sooner this is done after the show the better, for memories are then at their best for constructive ideas.

The final function of the committee is perhaps one of the most important and that is the provision of a proper statement of account – a balance sheet. This should be presented to the club membership at as early a stage as possible and should be properly audited by an independent person. Every payment, whether incoming or outgoing, should be clearly accountable and able to stand up to any scrutiny.

Delegation

Earlier (p.117) I mentioned the importance of delegation and would now like to elaborate on this further. Pigeon-show organisation, of course, is little different from real life as far as this matter is concerned and the successful and relaxed person is generally the one who is able to organise and delegate to people below him. This most certainly applies to the secretary of the pigeon show for the one who tries to do it all himself is bound to fail and to get flustered and worked up throughout the duration of the show with a resultant lowering of efficiency and overall success. I have seen this happen so many times that I am quite adamant about the absolute need for delegation.

The most successful shows I know are those which put great store upon delegation of responsibility within the overall organisation. It is then a simple matter for the secretary or the chairman to exercise control over the various personnel deputed to control the various facets of the organisation. The larger the show, the more need there is for delegation and division of responsibility and, in my view, the areas of responsibility usually take the following form:

(a) Secretarial Duties including the provision and despatch of schedules, the receiving and listing of entries and the despatch of pen numbers and other documentation. The financial side of the show may also be handled by the person responsible for the secretarial duties although, in larger events, the money side is best left to someone with a direct responsibility and possible expertise in this field.

(b) Judging Once the judges have been decided upon by the committee it is advantageous if one person is deputed to make the arrangements, including the expenses, refreshment and accommodation of selected judges.

(c) Draw or Raffle This is a self-explanatory fund-raising exercise necessary to most shows.

(d) Admission Where admission is to be charged, it is really best left to an individual to organise a rota of duty personnel at the door.

(e) Security – including the security of birds before, during and after a show. The safe-keeping of baskets and other show receptacles, of trade stands and of cash taken at the show.

(f) Care of the Birds – feeding, watering, cleanliness.

124

Figure 55. Inside the main hall at a major national pigeon show — the Old Comrades Show held annually in London.

(g) Refreshment Arrangements for both spectators and officials and judges at the show.

(h) Catalogue and Advertising Large shows may wish to provide a proper show catalogue, outlining the numbers and names of exhibitors in each and every class. The person who takes on this task may also assume the role of advertising officer, including press relations, both before, during and after a show.

There are other ways of dividing the tasks but, without doubt, a proper and true delegation of authority will aid in the overall efficiency of any pigeon show.

I would like to conclude by re-stating that it is the consideration given to small details that leads to overall success and I would like to urge any would-be show organisers to take particular note of this. Show organisers are generally pigeon fanciers themselves and therefore have a fair idea of what the exhibitor needs. Unfortunately, many of the classic shows seem to give scant regard to the exhibitor and, by so doing, they start to go wrong right at the outset. Concern for the comfort of the exhibitor and his birds will do much to enhance the standing of a show and its future. Those who have to travel long distances appreciate the availability of good show accommodation and of personal accommodation at suitable and reasonable rates.

It is good to see a show programme fully stated as in the schedule or on permanent display at the show. This should include timings of penning, judging, presentation of prizes and other events taking place at the show. Fanciers also like to see due attention being paid to security (see p.123). Exhibitors like to see their birds well looked after and they like to see timetables strictly applied, with prize cards, awards and prizes being promptly displayed.

Above all, exhibitors value fairness and impartiality at all stages of a show. This applies not only to the judging operation but to the whole event where the competition is open to all, from those who have travelled long distances to those who live in the locality.

I hope that the foregoing will be of interest and value to any show organiser. It goes without saying that the sport of pigeon showing is in need of good shows and of good and efficient organisers. For the organiser there is not only the prospect of hard work but also the considerable satisfaction of doing something which is valued and appreciated. A successful show which gives pleasure to exhibitors and spectators alike is also bound to enhance the standing of the sport.

Appendix:

The Showman's Year

This appendix is intended to be a ready guide to fanciers who show their pigeons and an aide-memoire throughout the progress of the year. To avoid too much repetition, I have divided the year into two-monthly periods. As it is, there is some duplication of advice but the information given for each period is comprehensive and can be treated as a separate article. It must be borne in mind that I have written for fanciers in Great Britain, so adjustments to the season will have to be made for other parts of the world. For novices in partiuclar, this should prove a useful source of information at all times of the year – to establish progress, to check the past and to plan for the future.

Showing is an art and, more often than not, success depends largely upon the amount of work and effort put into it. I think that this is borne out by the two-monthly divisions, which clearly indicate that, at all times of the year, there is work to be done in order to keep everything properly managed for showing needs. To successfully and enjoyably show pigeons, the work is necessary and the pleasure of winning greater when past efforts are remembered as being contributory.

I therefore hope that my thoughts on the necessities of life in and around the show loft will prove to be both stimulating and useful. The year encompasses much in any pigeon loft, from the peak of show condition to the production of the new offspring, to the moult and back to peak condition for showing. For convenience I commence with January, a peak month, and end at another peak in December. Between the two, however, much happens.

Part 1: January/February

The pigeon fancier's year never begins and ends with a date, for true fancying is an all-year continuous vocation. The months of January and February, however, are unique for the showman, for they mark the end of a season and the start of the process as it enters into another cycle. In these two months, the chances of success are either guaranteed or lost and, therefore, it is a very important part of the calendar and one which demands a fair amount of work but, above all, time and planning.

In January, the show pigeon is really at its best. The fitness stands out and the January shows are some of the most competitive of all. The moult is long over and forgotten and the birds, after a period of best diet for the show pen, are really on their toes and full of exuberance and glowing health. It is a real pleasure to visit show lofts during the earlier parts of January to witness what true show condition looks like.

The showman's sporting year ends with the January classics and while it should be remembered that these shows are very important, they also indicate the New Year's arrival and point to the task of planning for the next season. For many years, I rarely showed at the January events, preferring to devote the New Year to breeding activities but, nowadays, I like to think that I can, to some extent, combine the two tasks.

January is the month to take stock. With the Christmas rush over, the opportunity at last arises to sit down quietly and work out in a logical manner what has been achieved in the past season and what is required for the coming one. How have I done? Am I improving? These are the questions which have to be asked – and more important – answered.

Obviously, priority must be given to the remaining shows for which the birds are fit and to maintaining the condition of birds for as long as there are shows to be entered. Once the baskets have been put away for the final time though, thoughts must immediately turn to other things. Records are an absolute must for any fancier who wishes to achieve success and the record, of whatever form, must be as complete as possible. From this, assessments can be made of whether success has been achieved or whether there are faults within the team and places which need strengthening or improvement.

If it is necessary, then this is a reasonable time of the year to make purchases. Most successful fanciers are prepared to part with a bird or two at the start of the year in order to get down to breeding numbers and often very good birds change hands – birds which have served their owners well. Therefore, if a bird is needed to improve colour or type, or to go with a particular pigeon, then this is a good time of the year to acquire it. Such acquisitions must be made carefully, and after a good amount of thought, as too many 'imports' at this time can be detrimental to a team.

Panic often sets in at the conclusion of the show season when success has not come and all too critical looks are taken at the team. This is the time of danger for a team of show pigeons and one when a fancier must back his own judgement on its value. After all, it is his family of pigeons and he is the one to judge their merit. I have seen too many fanciers – often ones who should have learned by experience – go on a spending spree in order to buy another team when they think that theirs has failed them. This is where the long and patient study of the records will help, especially with regard to the potential of the young bird team. If the young birds have held their own in hard competition then there is little need to worry. If they have looked good in the pen, then it is folly to be stampeded into actions of disposal and acquisition which might be irreversible and damaging to future planning. Disappointments are hard to swallow but nevertheless they have to be encountered by us all. It is far better to meet disappointment with a determination to do better, based on what there is in the loft, than to have a mass importing session.

The message is therefore quite simple. Study now and success will follow later. Of course, it is not only the team as it stands at the end of the season that must be studied. Attention must be devoted to planning for the breeding season and also to deciding which birds to dispose of in order to reach breeding numbers. Both are serious matters and a lot depends upon the decisions made.

The selection of birds for breeding pairs is a subject in itself and all fanciers know of its importance. A lot of this work will probably have been done over the Winter months leading up to the end of the year, but January and February are the times when the final settling is done. I daresay that pieces of paper litter most pigeon households during the Winter period, bearing ring numbers and numerous lines and lists.

When pairings have been settled, then comes the time for reduction of the team to numbers suitable to embark upon the breeding process. One of the worst mistakes is to start breeding in a loft which is already overcrowded. To me, the saddest time of all is when making up my mind as to what to dispose of and this particularly applies when only a small team is kept. It is easy for the man with a stock loft where certain birds can be kept either on a temporary or permanent basis. However, the value of birds disposed of may be appreciated only when it is too late and this is where the danger lies. Empty perches are valuable and therefore numbers have to be trimmed accordingly and, however difficult and heartsearching the decisions are, they have to be made, and at the start of the breeding season is as good a time as any.

For those who practice early breeding and wish to show well on into the year, there are special difficulties. Early breeding in itself is an art, requiring a good settled environment and also a degree of luck. When it is coupled with showing, however, the problems are multiplied and the only real answer is to have two separate buildings in which to operate and, if possible, to have them out of sight and hearing of each other.

Not many showmen are able to do this and therefore the best has to be made of existing facilities. For the man with only two loft compartments, the combination of early breeding and showing form an almost impossible mixture. As soon as one or two pairs are mated, the rest get the urge to mate and they quickly go out of show condition. When I had a three-compartment loft, one of the partitions was always completely boarded and the birds in there were unable to see other birds in the loft. This was fairly successful for, while sounds obviously reached the unmated birds, their condition loss was nothing like when they were able to see the breeding pairs. This is probably the answer to those who wish to combine the two sides of the fancy during January, but great care must still be taken to avoid upsetting the show candidates.

Nest boxes must be installed with as little fuss as possible and, ideally, when the show birds are either away at a show or are basketed temporarily. It is a mistake to try to pair too many for early breeding if using only a part of the loft for the purpose. Three pairs at the most is probably a good figure and extra care can then be taken to see that the matings are made carefully and that the fighting, which all too often occurs, is avoided. Such sounds will excite the rest of the birds to distraction and a settled loft will be turned into one with a jittery atmosphere within a short while. I have made use of show pens quite successfully to get pairs to know each other. The object is to get them settled to their boxes and task as soon as possible and with as little fuss as possible.

Another advantage of using a compartment with solid partitions is that electric lighting can be used in that compartment without upsetting the rest of the loft. Light is most important to initiate early breeding which, after all, is being conducted at the darkest and coldest time of the year.

Before I turn to breeding in general as opposed to early breeding, a word or two about those January shows. The birds as stated earlier are at their peak and, in some cases, this means they might be carrying considerable weight. Most showmen work up a solid understanding with the teams and will be well aware of the birds with this problem. Some birds are liable to this more in January than at any other time and, therefore, care must be taken to see that such show candidates are weight-reduced to make sure that they have good balance. A fat bird will never handle correctly and no good judge will give it a second look.

Weight can be lost reasonably easily by placing the bird in a basket for a few days before a show but I consider this is somewhat unnatural and I much prefer a more gradual process or one which includes some of the basket work only. The object must be to get rid of the fat, but at the same time maintain condition and, more importantly, to encourage continuance of that condition for the show pen. The bird which is basketed for several days before a show may lose the weight but it may lose far more than that because of the treatment it has received. Generally, I use show pens for this purpose so that the bird to lose weight has water before it at all times, and daylight; I give it a very light feed daily – of, for instance, a few beans. Those which fly out will lose weight far more easily if they are given plenty of exercise.

For the rest of the birds with no weight problems, the matter is more straightforward and it is a question of keeping the condition going for the early shows. Plenty of bathing, good food and fresh water will see them through but I also favour use of a weekly tonic to keep the systems fresh. As there is a problem with the overweight, I find that young cocks are often a little under-bodied for the shows. I think that the young cock class at any show is often disappointing because of this factor. The young cocks are full of energy and spend their body heat on chasing about the loft. With the young cocks, it may be necessary to try to get a bit of weight on by adding more maize to their diet, together with small seed, but I would much rather try to remove weight than to put it on. I have even had five young cocks in a large compartment to themselves and still found it difficult to keep 'body' on them.

Personally, I enjoy the January shows for they can be entered using the full team at one's disposal. There is no problem of the moult and selection of the shows can be made using show condition as the main guide and it really is a pleasure having such a wide choice. In fact, decisions as to what goes to show and what has to stay behind can cause a great deal of head-scratching, and is just another example of the thinking that has to go into a team of pigeons during these first two months of the year.

When the shows are at last over, the showman's year overflows into the breeding season. Often the Sunday after the last show is labour day – the day when the loft is cleaned thoroughly and the nest boxes installed – or opened up. If proper care has been taken, pairings will have been worked out and matings can begin almost at once.

On the day of mating, I like to get the birds out on the wing, or into the flight and to give them a bath, for these two actions are wonderful ways of toning them up for what is to come. The main job is to cut weight down in all the birds to be mated and this is mainly done by reduction in corn but also through a change of diet to less fattening grains. The change-over should not be drastic but should be done with care and in easy stages. Nothing will scour a pigeon more quickly than a complete change of diet.

The importance of weight reduction cannot be overstressed and I believe that nearly every case of late-laying and other difficulties are due to overweight pigeons. For those who normally feed well it is not an easy task to give so much less but it is something which has to be done. I like the use of a mainly barley diet at this time for, after a high-protein-type feed, it is ideal to check body. A gentle purge will also pay dividends and do no harm to the birds.

Those who have fitted nest boxes in their lofts are at a real advantage when it comes to mating the birds. They are used to the boxes and, indeed, some pairs will merely take over the previous year's box. For those of us who install the boxes from year to year the problem is a bit bigger, but providing the installation can be done with little upset, the task will not be too great. My own boxes are in pairs and are complete, so can be put into the loft in a few minutes.

I like to keep as few pairs per compartment as possible for the fewer there are then the fewer the problems will be. In my own loft with 6×6 feet (1.8×1.8 metres) compartments, I allow a maximum of eight pairs and such a restriction really does help in getting the birds to settle to their respective boxes. A friend of mine puts all his breeding pairs into one compartment and, while it is large enough to house them all in comfort, the problems of settling are considerable and his first round always seems to produce a number of clear eggs. With only a limited number, individual attention can be given and this all helps in getting them to settle to the box.

Breeding is another subject and one which is deserving of special attention but a little thought at this time of year can solve a lot of problems. Before I leave the subject altogether, I think that the question of keeping adequate records of breeding is very important. It matters not what system is used so long as it is one which is foolproof, for memory in this respect is fickle. A small notebook kept in the loft will suffice and dates and ring numbers, etc., must be painstakingly recorded. I use small labels on each nest front and can well see that some sort of record card on each would be of great value. Never rely on memory for these important details. They should be put into the notebook as they occur and not left to chance. Not only dates but other observations recorded at the time will prove to be of value in the future.

When the birds are paired though, problems are often caused by spare cocks or hens, for it is not always possible to have even numbers. These can be a nuisance, the cock as a fighter and the hen as a flirter in enticing cocks away from the nest. The problem sometimes has to be met by isolating the offender(s) and it is something which has to be watched.

When showing is over, it is a good time to clean the show baskets out and to free them of chippings and sawdust. Sawdust in particular seems to cake if left. Ideally, the baskets should be stored elsewhere than in the loft and if possible on high shelves away from vermin. Mice or rats will quickly ruin baskets and will remain undisturbed for long periods if they are able to gain access. Baskets which are completely empty will be less inviting.

We often get fine days in the early months and these should be used to allow the birds to have a good fly whenever possible, following a bath. Birds certainly appreciate this and such liberations can do nothing but good. Easterly winds should be avoided.

Minerals and grit should always be available in the loft during the breeding season. It is amazing just how much of these are eaten at these times. Grit boxes are the easiest method of providing the grit but steps should be taken to see that it is always dry and clean. For this reason alone it may be best to give a few pinches of grit together with the corn everyday.

I see little reason to vary feeding habits during the breeding season so, if the birds are used to hopper-feeding, let them continue with it. I am not all that happy with a once-a-day form of diet when youngsters are being fed in the nest. Food should be before the adult feeders at least twice a day, and I personally prefer hopper-feeding during this time.

No matter how good the loft, extreme weather conditions will always drive the rain into a loft. I think that it is prudent, therefore, to take some sort of weather-resisting precautions early in the year. Whether showing is still in progress or whether breeding has commenced, the birds will do no good if they are subjected to a wet loft. Dampness is the enemy of good pigeon keeping. I therefore try to keep weather out by use of shuttering or other devices without destroying the value of the ventilation system. This can be done with common sense but I stress that it is better to do it early in the Winter than to do it only after the loft has been soaked or young birds killed through an icy wind.

January and February, although quiet months outwardly, are very important when one considers that what happens in the loft throughout the rest of the year relies to a large extent on decisions taken during this time. They are the months of planning and care to produce the foundation for future success.

Part 2: March/April

Any period of two months is a long time in the pigeon-fancier's year, but March and April see such a lot going on within the loft as to make them especially important. It is perhaps the one time of the year when there are no pigeon shows in the calendar, but nevertheless what happens in this period can determine the success or otherwise of the show team, not only during the coming season, but for several years ahead.

It is a time of the year which can experience the worst of the Winter weather and yet, in April, the weather can quickly change into long and settled spells of good conditions. Therefore, in this period, much of the management within the loft is decided by the weather conditions outside. As I have already mentioned, it is useless expecting good, healthy, early youngsters if the icy winds are allowed to blow through the loft unchecked and, while there is an absolute need for good ventilation, some measures must be taken to block direct and icy winds. Therefore, if some of the open areas to the front of the loft have been blanked off, it may be necessary to remove some of the wind proofing to allow for more healthy conditions inside when the milder weather arrives.

Breeding operations, of course, continue and those showmen who start early in the year, by March, are able to judge for themselves to some extent, the success or otherwise of the pairings. It is time to take stock and examine what is being produced, with a view to splitting and repairing certain birds. By so doing, years of planning and effort can be saved, in that a particular breeder, whether cock or hen, can be used with two, three or even four mates. Not only is this the best way to build a family around a proven producer but it is the best way of testing the potential of certain pigeons.

Such splittings are not easy and a great deal of thought has to go into each and every one. Ideally, it is useful to carry a few spare pairs to act as feeders, but those with small teams and lofts cannot really afford this luxury. The smaller the numbers breeding, therefore, the bigger are the difficulties. By astute switching of eggs and youngsters, this can often be accomplished without too great an upset to the loft. Eggs can be stored for up to seven or ten days, although they should be turned at least daily. A very good way to see that this is done is to put a cross on the side and to see that the eggs are turned twice a day; the cross should be facing upwards in the morning and downwards in the evenings.

The fewer numbers of young birds the adult pigeons have to rear the better, is a good general rule. Given the choice, I think I would restrict them to only two. The pigeon is a hardy and healthy creature and, providing that it is not overloaded too much, either physically or mentally, and by this I mean gross overwork, it is quite happy to breed and then enjoy a satisfactory moult before entering another show season. I am quite sure that, in my earlier years, I tended to rear too many youngsters from some pigeons, but now, with a balanced team, this is not so likely to occur.

Another way to take some of the stress off the show pigeon is to allow it to sit out a pair of dummy eggs after breeding is completed, so as to give it a complete rest. Birds are at their fittest in appearance when they have been sitting for ten days or so, and a continued period of sitting is useful for future condition. This is also useful when showing is to be practised into June and July, as a means of ensuring not only that the birds are exhibition-fit, but that their body moult is delayed too. This is a useful method of delaying the body moult for showing purposes within reason, but, once separated, the birds soon enter into a sudden casting of plumage.

The weaning of youngsters is another matter upon which there is considerable variation in practice. I tend to treat every case upon its merits and generally time it for about the twenty-first day. Before weaning, however, I like to ensure that the tail feathers are at least an inch in length and I use this as my real guide. Some wean much earlier than this while others allow the feeding to go on until about twenty-eight days. This, in my opinion, is far too long and is where the main stress occurs on the feeding parents. Common sense must be used and, during extreme frosty spells, the weaned young birds should be sheltered from the cold winds. I like to ensure that they are weaned in groups of four upwards, for company, warmth and guidance.

The quicker the young birds are weaned, the quicker they are likely to develop and fend for themselves. Once the initial check in development is overcome, they go along very well. Good food is so important at this time. Birds which are to be liberated should be allowed out of the loft as early in their lives as possible, and this is where a viewing cage is so useful. They are then able to view the surroundings as a first step to their general education. The first crop of youngsters always brings a few anxious moments when first released but, in my own experience, losses are very few. Bad weather over prolonged periods can spell danger here, for when the birds grow too strong on the wing before being allowed out, they then tend to be very erratic. Later on, towards the end of April, it is also very foolish to allow the youngsters out at weekends when old-bird training and racing is commencing.

As the adults start sitting out the second round of eggs, it will be noticed that the first primary is cast and the wing moult should then take an even and consistent course. The youngsters too, at this time, start to grow some of their new cover feathers and reveal their permanent plumage. Feathers at this time of the year are no problem for as soon as they blow out from the loft they are taken by the wild birds for their nesting material. I am always amazed at the variations in the methods of moult of the young birds: some go through the body moult very quickly, then tend to be late with their primaries, others do the reverse. It is a fact, too, that the March- and April-hatched youngsters catch up the earlier-bred birds in the moult and, in many cases, are full moulted earlier in the year.

Baths are important at this time of the year. Weatherwise it is not always a good time for bathing, especially where this has to be done inside the loft. The young birds in particular enjoy a bath and will tell you when they expect one by throwing drinking water around. Give baths as often as possible and, if the water is slightly warm, so much the better.

I mentioned feeding the youngsters when first weaned earlier and will now refer to feeding in general. I have always believed in feeding a good mixture during the breeding season and through the moult. Good sound pigeons will only develop fully when their feed is ample and wholesome enough and any skimping is false economy. Small seed is useful and I always have some available. During the moult, this is especially useful with a larger proportion of good linseed. Cod liver oil is a useful additive at these times. Some green food is also appreciated and so are mineral mixtures, whether in block or powder form. During the breeding season, this is greedily consumed. Grit is essential and must be always in front of the birds. Hoppers can be used for grit, or it can be given to them mixed with their corn supply. Youngsters must be given grit as soon as they are weaned.

While breeding is in progress, simple steps can be taken to see that insect life is kept away from the birds. An insecticide strip in the loft will eradicate most if not all insects, but, as an added precaution, insect powder can be sprinkled in the nest, under the bowl and in other parts of the nest box, or the loft can be sprayed with an insecticide substance. Simple precautions at this time of the year will solve most of the problems which might arise later on.

It is often very tempting to dispose of certain of the adults once the breeding season is getting to the end. With a full crop of youngsters, space becomes valuable and stock birds are often killed, sold or given away. I know that space is important, but it really does pay to wait a few weeks at least, to fully evaluate the youngsters produced. It is too late to regret the passing of a bird when suddenly realising the value of the birds produced. We have all done it. It is also a sound reason to ensure that the breeding season is entered with a basic number of birds.

At some time during the two months, the time comes when it is necessary to sit down and evaluate fully what has so far been achieved, with not only quality but also final numbers in mind. Numbers already reared have to be added to those being hatched and to that number must be added the numbers intended to be bred from certain pairings. The time comes when a halt must be called and it is useful to have an estimate of numbers as early in the year as possible. I carry out such an exercise at least once and generally twice during a breeding season and find it essential in making up my plans.

Records, too, must be kept up in an accurate fashion. A small loft notebook is essential and also some form of record on each nest box is desirable. Memory is fickle and should never be relied upon where breeding arrangements are concerned. For the showman, breeding to a family pattern, this is very important.

Pigeon fancying is a constant and almost full-time occupation and there is no season of rest if success is desired. It is a good idea to get into the habit of cleaning out and seeing to the basic chores, such as replacing drinking water and ensuring that there is no ice on it, every day. I personally like to have my nest boxes cleaned out regularly, though some never disturb the birds in this way. However, smells can soon develop and this is always more likely during the extreme cold weather when some of the loft front is temporarily blanked off. I have found that a second floor within each nest box is very useful, as this can be removed and scraped, or simply replaced with another floor. Sheets of hardboard the same size as the nest box are ideal for this. Alternatively, use clean newspaper to line the floor of each nest box.

During the breeding season thought must always be given to the culling of unsuitable youngsters. Early doubts are seldom wrong and, with ever-rising feeding costs, the aim should always be quality and not quantity. The stage at which birds are to be culled will vary with the breed, because mis-marks and faults are more obvious with some breeds than others, but with experience, the fancier will learn to recognise such matters. It is best to breed only from eggs which are clean, smooth and good-looking, discarding any which have rough shells, which are small or any way mis-shaped.

Likewise, in the nest, young pigeons which show any signs of distress, lack of growth or which are allowed to get chilled, may as well be disposed of as they rarely develop into healthy specimens.

The two months are important to any pigeon fancier. It is the one time of the year when showing takes a back seat to general requirements within the loft, although it is only through concentration at this time that a show team of merit is likely to be produced. The breeding season is important but it is the selection of the breeding pairs which is the most important subject. It is not a job which is done once in the year, i.e. before breeding commences, but one which should be borne in mind and studied right through the breeding operation. Never be afraid to experiment and split the pairings and try new ones. This is fanciership at its most crucial stage and, for the showman breeding to a family, the importance can never be exaggerated.

Part 3: May/June

If I had to pick a time of the year which I considered to be busiest within my loft, it would almost certainly be contained within these two months. It is a very exciting time, especially for those show fanciers who enjoy Summer showing. It is the time of the year when breeding is coming to an end and when it is possible to judge the success or otherwise of the breeding season. A few days away from the loft because of holidays or other cause, sees substantial changes in the young birds.

The month of May is when most show fanciers are finalising breeding arrangements. The vast majority of birds are hatched by this time, and birds bred much after the middle of May will probably be late in getting through the moult for the classic shows. Indeed, it might well be mid-November or even later before they are finally clear. As a fancier who starts showing in May, I generally aim to have the birds separated by the middle of May, and that entails having all the young birds weaned and everything cleared up to get the nest boxes out of the loft. In general, my last youngsters are hatched by mid-April. Occasionally, of course, through the splitting of pairings, or for other special reasons, I may be tempted to allow a pair or two to breed later in the year, but this is the exception rather than the rule.

To separate the pairs, however, is not necessary and, as I mentioned earlier, it is quite a good proposition to allow the pairs to sit out pot eggs, as a means of retarding the heavy body moult and producing good condition for important shows. However, many prefer a loft thoroughly cleaned out and without nest boxes, to condition the team for the early events. It is entirely a matter for personal choice. However, many fanciers keep their birds sitting on pot eggs; this is beneficial after a heavy rearing season as it affords the birds a period of rest.

Obviously, breeding programmes do not always go to plan and it might well be that breeding interferes with the early shows. I think, therefore, it is important to get priorities right in this matter. While I enjoy the Summer shows, they are certainly only sidelines and I would never forfeit young birds in order to be able to enter the parents at an early show. Every youngster is a potential champion and good birds could be lost merely by entering the parents at one of the early shows. Never forego breeding for the early shows.

Again it is a good idea to sit down and work out, on paper, the show programme. List the shows to be entered, together with possible teams in numbers and classification, and then work out the numbers available to show, bearing in mind breeding in progress. It may take time but it will be worthwhile. Generally, the Summer shows require entries to be made some time in advance and it is pointless entering numbers which cannot be found owing to breeding commitments. Planning is so important in every aspect and at every time of the year. This is just another example of how a paper exercise can reveal so much.

In my own case, showing starts in the middle of May and can continue into July, although every care will have to be taken that overshowing is avoided. Showing in the Summer is a worthwhile occupation so long as it is not overdone, otherwise the birds will suffer from fatigue, both physical and mental. There is then danger of a poor moult and lack of sparkle during the Winter when the condition most counts. Many newcomers to the showing side of the sport, and even fanciers of repute, tend to overshow. I know that in my first few years I did this, and in those days my team was not as comprehensive as it is today.

The importance of mapping out the shows to be entered and the birds used is very important. Bear in mind that the Summer events generally last for two days or more and, often being under canvas, are not ideal for pigeon showing. The stresses placed on the birds are many and, therefore, showing should be kept to a minimum in respect of each pigeon. Each is to be treated as an individual and such attention will always pay. If I had to set a limit, I would say that two shows, or perhaps three at the outside, in the three months from May to July inclusive, would be quite enough for a pigeon.

The main difficulty I have found is in writing for the many modes of management employed by fanciers. Up to now I have spoken a great deal about showing during this period, but there are plenty who do not bother with the Summer showing. Their requirements therefore are much different and less demanding. Breeding can be allowed to go along naturally with no need for thoughts of ending by a set date.

I have already written a fair amount about the splitting of pairs and it is not too late to do this during May and June, provided that it is realised that the youngsters produced will be rather late and may not get through the moult in the year of birth. There is nothing against late-breds but, again for the fancier with a small show team, these birds may well be passengers which cannot really be afforded. However, for the fancier with extra space in the loft, these two months may well be ideal for arranging some experimental breeding, for they are ideal months for the rearing parents.

I keep stressing the need for planning within a show loft, but during this time of the year, it is of the utmost importance. When breeding draws to a close, and we probably all breathe a sigh of relief when the last birds are weaned, there are many factors to be considered. Have I enough youngsters, is the quality good enough? Is it obvious that some of the pairings are producing quality, so that one or two more bred in the same way would be advantageous? These are the considerations and they can only be realised through much patient study.

Some fanciers are reluctant to handle their young birds but I have always made it a practice to do so. It is something to which they will have to get accustomed and it is only through handling that one can be made aware of obvious faults or deficiencies. It is also the surest way of achieving tameness and building an understanding. The youngsters change very quickly, sometimes for the better and sometimes revealing obvious deficiencies. Where there is the slightest doubt about a pigeon it is better disposed of. It is pointless carrying passengers which are unlikely to make the grade later on when the competition gets tough. Early doubts are rarely wrong and it is far better to cull early than to carry the birds which eat valuable corn and take up good perching and air space. However, some fanciers cull too early, being unwilling to await natural development, and this is a dangerous thing to do.

These decisions are for the fancier with a family of birds, for he will know more or less from precedent whether certain birds take longer to develop. The fancier with birds from here, there and everywhere is in a more difficult position, for he is unable to really anticipate what is to be produced.

An empty perch is often more valuable than the pigeon which might otherwise occupy it and the aim should be to reduce numbers as soon as possible and not to allow the overstocking situation to get out of hand. Not only must we consider the disposal of unsatisfactory young birds, but also of older and stock birds. There is always a temptation to get rid of some of those which have bred for us, but I would always advise that this be delayed for as long as possible. It is too late when a breeder is disposed of and its breeding value realised subsequently. Space has to be found in any loft at this time of year but it is sad when it is at the expense of a valuable breeder.

Just as it is a busy time within the loft, so it is in the house and garden. No doubt the finer weather will get the spring-cleaning and decorating going indoors and there is plenty to be done in the garden. Time for the loft, therefore, is often at a premium. However, the loft needs a good spring-clean and the conclusion of the breeding season is as good a time as any. Time must be found for this and effort spent at this stage on the necessary chores should be amply rewarded later on.

Having portable nest boxes, I am always pleased to see them finally removed from the loft. The debris left behind, such as feathers, can then be cleared out. If at all possible, I put a day aside for the work and, if this can be a good sunny and drying one, then so much the better.

Perches can be taken out and given a scrub and the walls and roof washed down with a disinfectant solution. For those who paint the insides of their loft – and I do not – this is as good a time as any to get the paint-brush going. When the final cleaning is done, the final touch is to spray the loft with an insect killer. It is a futile exercise to powder the birds the night before the first big show, for traces of the insect pests will be apparent for the discerning judge to see. Remember too that moths are at their most troublesome at this time of the year and a constant watch should be kept for them. They will hide in any convenient crack or other refuge and will play havoc with feathers during the night time. There are plenty of items on the market to banish the moth, such as sprays and repellent strips, and the small expense involved is well worthwhile. I have seen pigeons which have had a great deal of feathering eaten away by moths.

The long evenings are ideal times for the liberation of the birds and, in particular, the youngsters. I like to have them out as much as possible and at least once daily. It is always a good plan to let them out hungry so as to train them to return to the loft immediately after a flight, rather than to hang about on the roof tops.

Birds which are liberated fairly often from the loft, or allowed into a flight or aviary, are more easily conditioned than those which are kept prisoners. Plenty of baths too at this time of the year are ideal and, if these can be outdoors in the sunshine, so much the better. The moult by this time of the year is well in progress and some of the young birds which are earlier bred will be clearing up in body and will be ready for the shows.

With the moult very much in evidence, food is very important and it should be regular and constant. By this I mean that the quality should not greatly change and that periods between meals should not be too long. Green food is useful and grit too is taken readily. Water, of course, should be clean and the utensils scrubbed regularly. I also use a weekly tonic. In feeding, I keep to a varied mixture right through the breeding season and until the moult is clearing up.

Nest boxes and fronts should be thoroughly scrubbed and disinfected and, where necessary, painted. My portable nest boxes are taken out and scrubbed and then allowed to 'weather' for a week or two before being painted and put away. It is a job best done as soon after the end of the breeding season as possible, for the longer the task is put off, the more likely it is that it will be missed out altogether.

This is also a good time of the year to get necessary outside work done to the loft. Perhaps there are alterations to be done, or a new coat of paint is needed. Remember always that pigeon fanciers in general are judged by the general public on the appearance of their lofts.

I also use the good weather and long days for another chore, which I almost look forward to doing, and that is to thoroughly clean out the show containers. These are always scrubbed and hosed out, and when dried, are given a coat of varnish where necessary. I varnish mine every other year and find this one of the most rewarding jobs as the baskets can always put in to the shows with pride. Good show containers will last a lifetime if treated properly. If Summer showing is anticipated, it is a good thing to get them done before the first event.

I started out by warning that the months of May and June are among the busiest in the year. In my case, through my own system of management, they certainly are so. I seem to have little time for other things by the time the loft has been seen to. In the main, however, the hard work is rewarded not only by results, but by a sense of pride in knowing that everything is 'top line'. These 2 months are hard work physically and also mentally because of the effort of constant observation and study.

Part 4: July/August

In the two Summer months, the moult is the most dominant factor in the show loft, with management ensuring that the moult is a good one. If all the necessary work described for May/June has been done, there is little reason why July and August should not be restful ones within the show loft.

Good food, clean water and grit are the main requirements within the loft at this time of the year and birds so treated should condition themselves. The environment, however, should be as peaceful as possible. A few words about this rather mysterious factor would not come amiss. Environment in this day and age seems to be a fashionable word but, in this context, I am using it to mean 'atmosphere'.

A settled environment is something which is achieved sometimes by luck but more often by hard work and understanding. It is having a settled loft with quiet birds which do not appear to be on edge while either the fancier or visitors are present. There is no easy way of achieving this happy state, for it is something which has to be worked at. It is always a pleasure to enter a loft where it prevails, for there is a wonderful sense of order about everything.

Condition generally and a good moult are far more likely to be gained where the birds are settled and under control. It is appreciated that this state can be lost by quite small matters, such as one wild bird being introduced, or the birds being frightened but, in general, the fancier – bird understanding remains as a foundation for condition. I do not mean to put too much emphasis on this point because above all pigeons are hardy creatures and have the ability to put up with a great deal before health is adversely affected. We are, however, looking at the ideal.

Treat pigeons well but without fuss and the condition will surely follow. It is for this reason that I do not mind showing pigeons at the Summer shows. I have always done it and get great enjoyment out of these events. Even during the months of July and August, when the moult is at its height, it is possible to find a few birds to enter. Great care must be taken, however, to see that the birds are not overshown. It is a temptation to put the best out on every occasion, but if this is done, the birds will suffer from the stress and will fail to reach that peak of condition for the Winter shows.

I consider two or three shows enough for any pigeon in the months of May to July inclusive and, in addition, I do not like to show any pigeon more than once during July and August. By July, the moult is pretty well advanced and most of the adults are entering into the body moult. Youngsters, by this time, are starting to clear the moult, but few will be really show fit. Judging young birds during July is a daunting task, for in any class, only one or two will be anywhere near ready.

In the average loft, however, there will be a few birds clean enough in body to show. Even so, if the weather is hot, many will suddenly go into heavy moult and the pen and basket compartment will be lined with cover feathers. By August, however, the situation is even worse and even fewer birds are available for exhibition. Perhaps those which have not reared, or some which have been allowed to sit out eggs, will still be looking reasonably good in appearance.

It will be appreciated, therefore, that it is dangerous to overshow during these months and any novice should bear this in mind if tempted to do so. By all means have a go, but stagger the entry as much as possible, using different birds on each occasion. I enjoy the Summer showing but really it is only a side-line, for the competition tends to be confined to the few fit birds which are available.

Basic steps can be taken to see that those which are shown can recover from the period of stress. A bath upon return to the loft, and if possible a liberation, will soon restore condition and get the bird again settled. These are the small things which count so much for the showman and the show pigeons. For instance, if there is a team of birds away at a show, then in their absence it is a good idea for those left in the loft to have the bath. When the show birds return, they will be given the bath and will have it pretty well to themselves.

Enjoy the Summer shows by all means but be sure to see that the birds are only put out sparingly. Any show causes stress and during the Summer heat under canvas, this is exacerbated. It is the attention to detail in Summer which matters for Winter showing condition.

Rapid changes within the loft at this time of the year make it an interesting time. Holidays away from the loft will reveal big changes in the developing young birds upon return. It is important, when going away on holiday, to see that proper instructions are given to ensure that management during absence is as near normal as possible. A plentiful supply of the usual corn must be left to make sure that there is no enforced change of diet by changes in mixture or content. The less the person looking after the birds disturbs them the better and, therefore, cleaning can be kept to a minimum in this time. It is far better to have an experienced fancier caring for the birds. The experienced fancier would be able to spot any trouble, such as canker or one-eye cold, which, if unchecked for a fortnight, could ravage the whole team.

The return to the loft after an absence, however, is an exciting moment for the changes which will have taken place during the time will be quite substantial, especially with the young birds. Changes, of course, will be for the worse as well as for the better and, where this becomes obvious, the quicker the disposal of unwanted birds the better.

As the rate of the moult increases, it naturally follows that trouble with feathers increases. Daily, if possible, the feathers should be removed and disposed of in some permanent way. I keep a supply of paper or polythene bags available just for this purpose and then dispose of the feathers, contained in the bags, in the dustbin. Pieces of ply or hardboard, about a foot square, placed in the loft corners against the wall, at an angle of about 45° make useful feather traps. This is far better than having feathers flying about the loft interiors.

This time of the year is perhaps the worse for dust in the loft and all fanciers should take precautions to prevent it entering the lungs by using a mask. The dry loft in hot weather produces dust and the feather particles and pigeon bloom all add up to a danger. Avoid health problems by forming the habit of wearing a mask.

A good thing to examine during the Summer months is the state of ventilation. This is best tested either during hot periods or during those days when the atmosphere is muggy and damp. The best test is to note whether there is a stale smell pervading the loft. Ventilation is important at any time of the year and, in my opinion, most especially so during the Summer, when most lofts carry more pigeons than usually desirable.

There must be a means of allowing air in at a low level and giving it escape means at a high level — if possible on the opposite wall to the outlet. Many manufactured lofts now come with a foul-air escape built in at the rear of the loft and this is ideal, so long as it does not allow the rain in during wet periods. Louvres are ideal as inlets and are mostly of wood, although appliance manufacturers now supply them in metal or plastic form for fitting to lofts where the ventilation is inadequate. The type which can be closed or opened at will are best.

It goes without saying that, as the moult progresses, frequent baths are vital to the birds. The more baths, the better the moult is likely to be. The water helps the feathers to grow naturally and there is little doubt that, health-wise, the birds benefit a great deal from bathing. Small seed, including good linseed should be given, although in moderation so as not to upset the balance of the natural moult. Water will have to be changed daily or more often; this is more essential with feathers blowing into it. It is a good idea to get the drinkers up off the floor and a good-sized shelf is useful.

During the moult, it is essential for the showman to see that steps are taken to eradicate insect life on the birds. There are various methods for this, but action must be taken. I think most of us nowadays use the products on the market to spray the lofts out twice a year. Others prefer the use of aerosols or powders, but one useful method is to employ insect repellent strips. Providing these are changed in accordance with the manufacturer's instructions, they will rid the loft of red mite and other pests. As I have already mentioned, precautions should also be taken against moths, which if unchecked will cause considerable feather damage.

Empty perches are valuable. A settled environment will never be attained if there is a shortage and the birds spend half their time fighting for perches. During the show season, a good guide is two perches per pigeon but, as fanciers, we know that, during the Summer, following a full breeding season, this is not always possible. We all keep a few extra birds because it is not until after the moult that we are able to sort out those to be kept for the show team and those which can be disposed of. However, the rule should be to reduce numbers as much as possible and as soon as possible.

For those birds with obvious faults, the matter is easy, but all sorts of considerations have to be taken into account. Breeding potential and value, family pattern, colour, shape, size, are all matters which have to be borne in mind.

And so we have the months of July and August – the season of flying feathers. The main aims should be to keep the food and water clean, give plenty of baths and keep the lofts clean. Reduce numbers as soon as possible and, where showing is done, see that it is kept to a minimum. A settled and ordered environment is the best recipe for success.

Part 5: September/October

The year continues and, within the loft, we see the time when the moult is at its worst. These are the months of bedraggled-looking birds, which tend to be less exuberant than usual. Little wonder, for the changing of the feathers must bring with it a fair amount of strain.

For the previous two months, I stressed the importance of having a settled environment during the period of the moult and this is a useful way to begin here. If we accept that a certain amount of stress is imposed upon the birds during the moult, then the better the conditions are within the loft, the better chance there will be of the moult passing without undue strain. I do not suggest that any unusual steps should be taken, merely that the way is cleared to get the settled atmosphere within the loft. Cleanliness, with good food and water, contribute largely to this, but will be wasted if the loft is so overcrowded that there is a constant battle for perch and air space. Likewise, if ventilation is inadequate for numbers kept, there is less chance of an uneventful moult.

This was forcefully brought home to me when I purchased a small garden shed to use as a stock loft. It was a conventional shed and had to be converted for use by the birds, but being busy this work was postponed somewhat. Then, one wet and muggy day, I entered the shed to find the atmosphere within most unsuitable for pigeons. Compared with my main loft, where the ventilation was excellent, the shed was a breeding ground for disease. Ventilation is of the utmost importance and should be corrected before anything else is done within a loft. As previously mentioned, a mask should be worn as often as possible in the loft and most certainly when cleaning out.

At this time of the year, the aim should be to reduce numbers in accordance with the amount of space and perch accommodation available. It pays to be somewhat ruthless over this and I can only repeat what I have said previously, that an empty perch is often as valuable as the bird occupying it. Numbers kept at this time of the year are bound to be over and above the normal, for it is necessary to see birds through the moult before making final decisions. Nevertheless, thoughts on reduction must always be present. The fancier who already had too many birds at the commencement of breeding operations will now find the loft even more overcrowded and will have the most problems. Do not make that mistake and always strive to keep to the pre-determined size of team.

Make sure that the environment within the loft is correct and the moult should be a good one. Maintain the feeding as usual and ensure that there are no sudden changes in content, for a complete change of food or mixture will often cause upset, which might result in feather fretting. I use a varied mixture during the moult and always couple this with some small seed, especially linseed. This should be fed sparingly as over-fatness should be avoided.

I allow my own team freedom from the loft whenever weather conditions allow. They will fly only as much as they wish and I am quite convinced that good sunlight is very beneficial. Likewise, good hard rain showers will give the birds a lot of satisfaction and pleasure, and surely this is what I am talking about – giving them conditions they enjoy.

Before leaving this particular subject, I can do little better than to commend readers to the work of the late Dr W. E. Barker entitled *Pathway to Success*. This little article contains a great deal of truth and it says, in effect, what I am trying to say. I quote:

'A bird to be successful in such an ordeal as I have supposed about must have eaten good food at regular intervals, have drunk pure water constantly, have breathed pure air habitually. Here then is the clue for the would-be successful fancier, namely regularity. It implies much more than the precise meaning of the word conveys. The man who is methodical and does things regularly, not only does them regularly but ninety nine times out of a hundred does them well. A man who feeds regularly is pretty sure to use the best food obtainable; the man who sees to a constant supply of fresh water and is careful too as to the cleanliness of the vessels containing it. The man who cleans out his loft regularly will clean it thoroughly and this man, though success may be delayed and seem hard to win is sure as certainty goes in this world to make his mark in the long run and having gained the summit he is, to use an expressive phrase "bad to shift".'

September and October within the show loft are the months of the 'big build-up' towards the classic show season. To the serious showman, all efforts are directed this way and all the work is aimed at producing birds for the classics which are fit and right for the judges. Just as September sees the birds at the lowest in appearance through the moult, by the time October draws to an end, most are through the body moult and looking well in their new covering.

Showing of course is carried on throughout the two months, although during the early part of September it is not really practical. By mid-September, however, there are a few shows and the young birds are fit and ready for them. The adults which are fit enough to show, however, are few and far between. The shows, therefore, are good venues for the youngsters because, being of a local nature, they are ideal training grounds for the young pigeons.

Pen training is very important in my opinion and I would always advise that every young pigeon is so trained before it is put out in a real show. If this is not possible then a little local showing is very valuable in this respect. The training should be as complete as possible, with birds being basketed, penned, judged and re-basketed before return to the loft. This is essential grounding. It is wrong to show a young pigeon for the first time ever, say in a two-day classic show, and expect it to stay in condition afterwards.

Showing for the untrained pigeon is a considerable ordeal and it is likely to lose so much condition in a two-day show that it will take several days to sufficiently recover for future events. The old stagers take it all in their stride but the picture is different for the newcomers to shows. Therefore I always stress the importance of pen training at home, or certainly at local-type shows.

With the show season fast approaching, steps should be taken to ensure that show containers are in first-class condition. These jobs should have already been done but better later than never. See that the containers are clean and contain a good layer of either chippings or sawdust. I prefer the latter, although a mixture of the two is quite satisfactory. The material must be kept clean and it is advisable to change the contents completely after every two shows, especially where the birds have spent considerable periods in the containers.

If changes are planned for the loft, it is time to get them done but whatever changes there are, they must be completed as long as possible before the commencement of the show season. It is useless to expect condition in the birds if they are being subjected to changes within their loft. We are back to the settled environment and birds, like human beings, tend to be conservative and resent change. What pertains in the loft at the start of the show season, should be so at the end of it.

Feathers should be collected and disposed of daily and this is as good a time as any to get the loft sprayed inside to kill off any unwanted insect life. I like to do mine at least twice a year but even if this is done, complacency should never be allowed and constant attention should be paid to the birds to make sure that red mite and other insect life does not appear. Providing that the simple precautions have been taken throughout the year, there should be no trouble. Dusting powder in the nest bowls during the breeding season and then a couple of sprayings should be enough. This, however, should be coupled with other factors, such as seeing that the loft is kept clean at all times and the walls washed and kept clean also.

The importance of cleanliness cannot be over-emphasised and, with the approach of the show season, this is doubly important. The loft should be cleaned at least once daily and if possible twice. This is where I find the shelves underneath my perches very useful because they can be scraped clean in a matter of seconds and, as they catch the majority of the droppings, the loft is rarely allowed to go long without being cleaned.

Baths should be given as often as the birds want them but, when the showing starts, it is advisable to give them a few days before actually showing the birds. Inevitably, some of the bloom is removed and it takes a day or two for it to be replaced, even in a pigeon in the fittest of condition. In the height of the season, my birds are given a bath weekly – generally on Sundays, but sometimes a second one is given on Tuesday or Wednesday.

I must return to the numbers to be kept in the loft. Thoughts must be constantly turned to possible ways of reducing the team. This can only be done by observations of the birds in the loft, of their behaviour, appearance and type. The two months in question see great changes in individual birds, but by the end of September, it should be possible to have a very good idea on which is likely to stay or to have to go. This is not a 5-minute job and can only be done after hours and hours of patient work. It is this work, coupled with a profound knowledge of the family pedigree, that makes the job of selection anything other than a 'hit-and-miss' affair. I find it the hardest part of the pigeon year and the temptation to retain more birds than is advisable is very great. Unless the temptation can be overcome, the sure result is an overcrowded loft.

It has often been said that the art of pigeon keeping is in the breeding and, while I agree with this, I am inclined to think that equally important is the art involved in selecting permanent members of the show team. Considerations are many and varied. Show potential is obviously a main one, but so too is future breeding planning. Brilliant show birds do not always make the best breeders and, in my book, they never do – at least until they prove to me that they can. In other words, I tend to treat them as extras over and above the main core of the breeding team until they produce something good in the nest. The breeders, however, are valued and I daresay that, given a choice between the up-and-coming star and the proven producer, I would keep the latter at the expense of the show bird every time. This is my own guide but it is a matter for each and every individual fancier and, in this alone, he will stand or fall as a show fancier of repute.

With the coming of the classic show season, one thing is very important and that is to keep rain out of the loft. A dry and waterproof loft is essential for show pigeons and steps should be taken to see that the rain is not allowed to drive in because, if it is, the birds will certainly lie about in the wet patches and this is the surest way of getting them soiled. Cocks tend to get their tail feathers dirty and it is little use sending them to shows in this state. Baths are the best way of getting them clean. However, individual feathers can be washed in a warm and mild soapy solution and then thoroughly rinsed – the latter is very important. The birds can be placed in a clean show container in a warm place to dry, or a hair dryer may be used for this purpose. The electric dryer seems to dry the feathers quite naturally and afterwards the job done should be impossible to detect.

The showing of pigeons at this time of the year is not the easiest of operations because of the varying states of the moult within the loft. Youngsters, having nearly finished the moult, are able to be shown, but most of the adults will be looking bedraggled right up to October. The individual attention to birds in the show team therefore is very difficult and will have to be done away from the main loft. For instance, the bird which is fat will have to be weight-reduced by using a basket or pen. As long as the moult is on, it is of the utmost importance that the birds are fed and watered regularly. If they are allowed to go for a long period without food, fret marks are likely to appear and this will detract from chances of show success. The bird to be reduced in weight will, therefore, have to be kept penned and fed only very lightly, although it should be given access to water at all times. I am very much against keeping birds in show containers for days on end without food, as I am quite sure that this is cruel. I generally use the pen in the following manner. The bird(s) to be weight-reduced are taken out of the loft at feeding time and placed in a show pen where they are given a very small amount of food – generally beans or peas – just enough to keep the stomach occupied. After the other birds have eaten, the 'treated' birds can be returned to the loft. This is a painless and humane way of doing an important job within a show team. The same method, but in reverse, can be used for birds which require more weight, without doing the same to the rest of the show team. I use small seed and maize as a means of adding body weight.

I began by describing the September/October period as the 'big build-up'. This it is, for what matters in any show loft, is the success or otherwise gained during the classic show season. The 2 months in question have seen the transition of a team from a group of birds heavy in moult to a good-looking and fit team for the shows to come. A lot of work will have to be done in this time but it is mainly work that the fancier with regular habits will take in his stride and, in any case, accept as being the norm.

The show season should be treated like a campaign. As in every other aspect of pigeon fancying, there should be a planned course of action. 'Campaign' seems a high-flown word, but it suits ideally the task to be undertaken within the show loft. Plan on paper the shows which are to be entered and the size of team envisaged for each. Then put on paper the numbers of birds available for each of those shows, bearing in mind the differing stages of the moult. The birds should be allocated to four divisions: adult cocks, adult hens, young cocks and young hens.

Only by working out a programme in this precise way will it be possible to present a well-balanced team on every occasion and to avoid overshowing. Coupled with this, there will be other considerations, such as the time which the birds will have to spend away from the loft, either in pen or container, and the amount of travelling to be done. Birds for the show pen are very hardy but there is a limit to the amount of strain they can take owing to travel and showing. Birds going out only to shows of a local nature can be shown far more often than those subjected to travel and to crowds.

It is a matter for a lot of thought and planning and only by this will the birds be fit and ready for the shows, to be entered with any hope of success. This is the 'build-up' and, in the next stage, we will take a look at the last period of the year – the one which really matters to all serious showmen.

Part 6: November/December

At last we have arrived at the highlight of the showing year. The two months when showing is at its best, with the classics and the club shows providing some of the best competition. The birds by now should be at their very best and it is a wonderful sight to see teams of superbly fit show pigeons within a loft.

By the beginning of November, the moult will pretty well be over and most of the birds will be looking at their best in new feather covering. Even so, there will be differences within a loft, with some adults still finishing off the primary moult and growing the last of the tail feathers. Those which have not reared any youngsters are often that bit further behind in the moult, having started later in the year than those which have been paired.

Youngsters, almost without exception, will be looking fine bodily but the later-bred birds will be clearing up the primary moult. By later-bred, I mean those hatched from mid-May onwards which may still be carrying a nest flight or two, and real late-breds will often as not, fail to get through the primary moult in the year of breeding. The moult is a fascinating subject in itself and there is no set cycle. Birds bred in March and April often moult out faster than those bred in January and February, which sometimes enter a secondary body moult. The task of feather collecting is, however, by this time of the year, getting easier but it should not be neglected. It is a good rule to keep a paper bag handy and to scoop up loose feathers daily. It is good to be rid of them.

Loft cleaning is now more essential than at any other time of the year. Some sort of set routine is essential to ensure that the loft is scraped and cleaned at least once daily, and preferably more. Nowadays I scrape out first thing in the morning and then, later in the day, it is only necessary to do the job quickly. Loft cleaning should be done often, as this can mean less work in the long run. However, any sort of presence by the fancier in the loft is useful as a means of building a relationship between fancier and birds. There is no substitute for time. It is also worth reminding fanciers of the need to protect one's health by the wearing of a mask when in the loft and certainly during cleaning operations.

The aim should be to minimise the chances of the birds soiling themselves on loose droppings. Other basics are as in other months – plenty of clean water in clean receptacles. A daily change of water is preferred and the drinkers should be thoroughly cleaned at least once a week. With birds going to shows and being mixed with other birds, the importance of precautions against disease cannot be overstressed. Therefore, emphasis must always be on loft cleanliness and there are plenty of good products on the market to add to the safety.

I also think it useful to add a suitable tonic to the water now and again. Again there are brands on the market which are good. A small amount of iron sulphate can also be added to the water – just enough to colour the water is quite sufficient.

Food at this time of the year in the show loft is very important, as is the method of feeding. One of the main things is to be regular in habit and to stand by practices started at the beginning of the show season. Decide on the food to be given and then ensure that there is a sufficient supply to last the season. It is inadvisable to switch mixtures in mid-season as upset can easily be caused resulting in lost condition. I can well remember once switching from a varied mixture to one containing nearly all beans and could not understand why the birds were lacking weight and losing form. That year, I was panicked into buying a bag of good maize in an effort to restore weight, but it was a losing battle and the weight was of the wrong kind in any case, being soft instead of good and firm. Therefore the message is really quite simple – keep to the usual mixture and if you want to convert from feeding for the moult to feeding for the show pen, then bring about the change in a gradual manner. Nowadays I keep to a good mixture, the only difference being that I step up the pea and bean content during the height of the season.

I have constantly mentioned the importance of the settled environment within a loft and consistency of diet is an intrinsic part of this. Change the food suddenly and there is danger of upsetting the settled or accepted state within the loft. These are the small matters which often mean so much to management, but pigeons, like human beings tend to dislike change. Indeed, when attending shows it is a good idea to carry some of the usual food mixture to feed the birds in their pens. Some fanciers even carry water for the same reason.

Get the birds to be happy within their own loft and they are likely to condition themselves. Fanciers know what a difference occurs if the birds are suddenly upset or put on edge by some outside danger, such as the presence of a cat. The settled state within the loft is the main ingredient in achieving condition. On fine days, I think it a good thing to get the birds flying out and I am sure that this contributes to keeping them happy. It is appreciated that many showmen do not liberate their birds, either through choice or because circumstances do not permit it. In such cases, a flight will allow the birds to get out into the sunlight and open air. Although most of my birds are allowed out, there are some prisoners and I must say that these never seem at a disadvantage in condition compared with those allowed to fly. However, when we are talking in terms of the final peak of condition, and keeping pigeons at that peak, then the hour or two they are out on the wing makes just that little difference in mental outlook. After being away from home for a couple of days showing, the birds appear to appreciate a bath and being allowed out. These are the small matters which make up the whole.

When dealing with October as the month leading into the show season proper, I laid stress upon the necessity of planning the whole of the season and used the word 'campaign' to describe it. This is very important and it is very necessary to plan, down to the finest detail, the shows to be attended and the numbers available for entry. Overshowing must be avoided but this is where the preparatory work means so much. Birds which have been consistently fed a good diet will be far more likely to keep in condition than those which are suddenly fed good grain upon the outset of the showing season. I am sure that this also applies in the racing lofts. There are too many part-time fanciers who, when their particular season is over, tend to sit back and relax. There is no time for this, for fancying is an occupation lasting for the full 12 months.

Birds which are supremely fit can be shown for several consecutive weekends without losing weight or condition. Providing that the ground work has been put in, the birds will stand up to a fair amount of showing, although again what applies for one bird may not pertain to another and this is where the individual observation is so essential. Young pigeons especially must be carefully watched.

By 'several consecutive weekends', I mean two or three, and perhaps even four, but this will depend a great deal on the type of shows and the time the birds are expected to stay away from the loft. The man with the smaller team will certainly be able to keep a close watch on the birds and see that no strain is being imposed. Therefore the planning might very well allow for successive shows to be entered so long as a halt is called at an appropriate time. Therefore, during the height of the showing season, shows can be entered for the three or four weekends, but there should then be a complete rest of at least a fortnight, i.e. one blank weekend, before an important classic.

The conditioning of birds for the show pen is a continuous process and runs from show to show without a break. I will give a small example of this. When I am showing birds away, or sending them, I arrange for the remainder of the birds in the loft to be given a bath in the absence of the team. Therefore when the team arrives back home and are given a bath, they are likely to have it all to themselves, without the usual pushing and shoving for position. Likewise, I try to make it a rule that, whatever time I arrive back from a show, the birds are put back in the loft so that, when the morning comes, they are in familiar surroundings. Small things really, but when added together, they constitute condition of mind and body.

The birds give us all a great deal of pleasure and therefore a small amount of work and effort in return is not out of the way. Treated properly and with common sense, the birds will condition themselves and all the work put in will be repaid with interest in the pleasure of knowing that the team is fit and right.

Records are valuable in the formation of a plan for the show season. It is worth knowing the success or otherwise of birds under certain judges and, in this way, it is possible to follow a judge using the same birds, or those of similar type. Colour forms an essential part of this, for it is well known that some judges favour birds of a particular colour. One may remember that a judge likes birds of, for example, a larger type. In general, I think it is fair to say that most judges select birds of the type kept by them and this is a reasonable guide. This is just one aspect of how records can assist but there are many more and every show should be faithfully recorded, as should the performance of every pigeon in the loft. It provides an insight into the loft and inmates, and also gives hours of satisfaction in reading and studying at a later date.

Although this is the height of the show season, it is also the time when plans are being made with regard to future breeding. Breeding operations do not merely happen, they have to be planned and worked at. The show team for instance will probably be a little bigger than the size of the team to be kept for breeding pairs. Unless there is a certain reduction at the end of the show season, it is only too probable that the breeding season will be entered with too many birds.

Most of us spend more time than ever with our birds during the show season and therefore we are constantly observing them, not as show specimens necessarily, but with future potential in mind. The show pen is a useful guide for this, for type is one of the main considerations when pairing up, and type becomes more apparent than ever when the birds are studied in the pen.

Now, let us consider the process of actually showing. The pre-show period is perhaps the most important, for the work done leading up to the show will pay dividends. In poor weather, it is a good idea to place baskets in a warm place to ensure that they are properly aired and free from dampness. Allow plenty of time for the pre-show checking period. It is no use keeping show pigeons throughout the year and then to skimp the final preparation. Great thought will have to go into which bird is to be entered, but this has probably been decided before basketing starts. It may well be, however, that the last-minute check reveals certain matters which lead to substitutions being made. However, once the birds are in their containers, then follows the time-consuming but very necessary process of checking the birds.

Each bird must be carefully checked. The examination must be very thorough, as though the birds are being judged at the show. Any trace of dirt or soiling should be removed and feathers checked for damage of any kind and, of course, for insect life. Bottoms of the feet should be clean, although it is not desirable to scrub the feet – as was the practice in past years. The ring/band number of each pigeon should be carefully entered on the compartment label. This is an essential thing to do in the interests of safety of the exhibit and to assist show organisers in sorting out mistakes which occur from time to time. This period of final checks might take some hours depending on the size of team intended to enter. I generally do it with a bowl of warm water available, a kettle of boiling water – to steam out damaged feathers, and a good dry towel. Every minute so spent however, is likely to be repaid in the show hall.

If the birds are basketed the day or evening before the show, it is also a good idea to make one final check the following morning before travelling to the show, i.e. open each compartment and carefully remove the accumulated droppings in the basket. This will considerably reduce the risk of feather soiling during the journey.

On the subject of the journey, make sure that plenty of time is allowed for it and any possible delay which might occur during it. It is important to allow plenty of time between penning and judging to give the birds a chance to get used to their surroundings and to settle. All the preparation is wasted if one arrives too late for judging or with insufficient time to allow the birds to settle.

And so the year ends really as it started – in the classic show season. This is a wonderful time of the year for the birds, which are looking at their best and wonderfully fit. To summarise, my concluding advice is exactly the same as for any other part of the calendar – clean lofts, clean air, good food and clean water. This, coupled with regularity and sensible treatment, must surely bring about condition, and this is what is needed to win at any pigeon show. Good showing.

Index

Numbers in *italics* refer to illustrations.

Picture Credits

Some of the black and white photographs were provided by the author, Douglas McClary. Other sources, which the author and publishers gratefully acknowledge, are listed below.

A. Bolton: p. 103
Alan Beaumont: pp. 96, 97, 98, 99, 100, 101, 104, 105
Michelle Burley: pp. 102, 108, 109, 113
Rick Osman: pp. 19, 24, 36, 69
E. L. Robbins: p. 20
Tom Smith: p. 30
Iain Wight: p. 15

The line drawings were specially prepared by Anita Lawrence.